ROAK

Sam Quek MBE is an internationally successful field hockey player who was a vital member of Great Britain's women's hockey team that won the gold medal at the 2016 Rio Olympic Games. This was the first ever Olympic gold medal for Great Britain's women's hockey. Sam is now a full-time presenter of the BBC's daytime TV show *Morning Live* and in 2021 presented the Tokyo Olympics live on the BBC. Also in 2021, Sam became the first ever female team captain on *Question of Sport*.

Sam lives with her husband and their two children.

ROAR

A CELEBRATION of GREAT SPORTING WOMEN

SAM QUEK

WITH HELENA DRAKAKIS

ALLEN&UNWIN

First published in hardback in Great Britain in 2023 by Allen & Unwin, an imprint of Atlantic Books Ltd.

This paperback edition first published in Great Britain in 2024 by Allen & Unwin, an imprint of Atlantic Books Ltd.

10 9 8 7 6 5 4 3 2 1

A CIP catalogue record for this book is available from the British Library.

Paperback ISBN: 978 1 83895 917 3
E-book ISBN: 978 1 83895 916 6

Printed in Great Britain by Clays Ltd, Elcograf S.p.A.

Allen & Unwin
An imprint of Atlantic Books Ltd
Ormond House
26–27 Boswell Street
London
WC1N 3JZ

www.atlantic-books.co.uk

To my daughter Molly, I dedicate this book to you with hope that the tenacity and dedication of the amazing women noted within its pages inspire you to do great things.

May their trailblazing make your own sporting path, should you choose to take it, that much smoother.

(And to my son Zac, I love you just as much as Molly, but I dedicated this book to her specifically, as you were born at a time when women's sport still struggles to achieve parity with men's sport. Hopefully by the time you are old enough to read this book, things will be on a much more level playing field.)

Contents

Gabby Logan MBE

TV presenter

When Sam asked me to write the foreword for *Roar: a Celebration of Great Sporting Women* I was delighted. I'll never forget travelling to work at the athletics stadium at the Rio Olympics in 2016. We were all glued to our phones watching Team GB winning that women's hockey final. It pushed the *News at Ten* back – very little manages to do that – and I remember saying to my colleague Denise Lewis that it felt like one of those big seminal occasions in women's sport. Feeling the enormity of that powerful national moment and witnessing the infectious team spirit of which Sam was a part was really something special.

It's achievements like that which have incredible resonance in all sport, but it's been brilliant for me to have witnessed throughout my career the rise of more of those awe-inspiring moments in *women's* sport. As a schoolgirl I was a competitive gymnast before moving into broadcasting full-time after I graduated from university in 1995. To say the landscape was different back then would be an understatement. We watched women playing tennis, competing on the athletics track and playing golf at a high level with some of the attention their male counterparts enjoyed, but equal visibility across a wider range of sports was a long way off.

Even in my profession, there was a prevailing idea that sport and sports presenting was a largely male space. If women weren't seen competing then why would we want to talk about sport? I guess I was lucky that when I debuted on Sky Sports it was at a time when the door was opening for women, if only slightly. I wanted to show viewers that not only could I do my job well, but also that women could have an interest and a passion for sport and that door could be opened further.

Yet as I write this foreword in 2023, I doubt even I could have imagined that I'd ever witness the Lionesses storm to victory in the 2022 Women's European Championship with the top peak TV audience of the year – a record 17.4 million in the UK. Or, that only last week I'd be standing on a freezing-cold touchline at the women's Six Nations rugby tournament in front of a sell-out crowd. A decade ago women's teams would have played to a handful of spectators – one man and his dog, I joke. Now the atmosphere is electric, the quality of play is fierce and the momentum behind women's sport is accelerating fast.

None of this has come easily. It wasn't until I began presenting women's football in 2007, for example, that I started to educate myself fully about why, when I was growing up, girls weren't seen playing football. A fifty-year ban – more of which you'll read about in this book – prevented us from doing so. Yet the more the game has received coverage, plus the support and investment that has been channelled into it, the more it has flourished. This model for success is now trickling down to other sports, whether it's team games or individual categories. Admittedly progress has felt like a giant tanker turning, but thankfully a sea change is happening.

Positive action has underpinned that change. The introduction of National Lottery funding in 1997 for elite sport was a game-changer for women. On the back of that investment, the London 2012 Olympics created many female role models and highlighted sports – such as cycling and rowing – where traditionally women were not celebrated. The impressive female medal haul that followed meant women could no longer be ignored. Women's sport was no longer the poor relation. Instead, it was a force for good. Investing in women could no longer be a box-ticking exercise. Instead, it was a huge opportunity for governing bodies, sponsors, broadcasters and fans to champion women – it's an opportunity I believe will be unlocked further in the future.

I've also experienced a cultural shift. Sport is tough and elite sport is *really* tough. There's no easy way to the top. Arguably society has protected girls from the rough and tumble of sport – the highs and lows of competition involve getting hurt both physically and emotionally. Yet what the world is starting to see is that women can inhabit that space, but do it in their own unique way and on their own terms.

Moreover, questions are being asked over access to sport which has more commonly been better for boys, whether that's at school or within the local community. Inspired by national successes in a range of disciplines and the ensuing enthusiasm of daughters, grand-daughters, nieces and sisters, more people are asking what's available for girls.

Every woman featured in this book, including me and Sam, started out by simply loving sport. And, as you'll read, sport isn't all about the elite level. Although the stories in this book provide an honest, at times gritty yet exhilarating insight into elite competition, each woman's experience is about so much more than that. Sport is about being mentally fit and healthy. It's about overcoming hardships; it's about developing self-confidence and self-esteem. It gives us the best life lessons about how to work in a team, how to cope with failure, and how to bounce back and achieve success. It's about knowing that when we put the effort in, we get so much out.

Having got to know Sam since her 2016 Olympic success, I understand how she found her own confidence through sport, and how passionate she is about being a positive role model and an ambassador for women's sport. The stories she has gathered here are vital to our understanding of women's sporting history – where we've come from and where we are going – and will resonate way beyond these pages.

Gabby Logan

We Can Do Anything

Sam Quek MBE

HOCKEY PLAYER

In 2016 I stood on an Olympic podium with fifteen teammates united in one crazy, unbelievable moment. As a member of the British women's hockey team, we had just won a historic victory again the Dutch to take the gold medal at the Rio Olympics. The nerve-shredding adrenalin of a match decided on penalties was still coursing through me as the noise of the thousands-strong crowd exploded around the stadium.

At the game's climax it was our defender Hollie Webb who stepped up to take the final penalty shot. Everything we had worked for as a team, everything we had practised time and again in training, rested on eight short seconds. It felt like a lifetime. As she dribbled right, then left towards the Dutch keeper, finally landing the ball in the back of the net, disbelief, joy and relief flooded through me. With my arms wide open, I ran towards my teammates and we hugged and jumped and danced. Afterwards, when I scanned the stands to find my mum, dad and my now-husband Tom, they were standing with tears streaming down their cheeks.

For the fans at the Deodoro Stadium that day, plus the ten million people watching on TV around the world, it was a tournament that became the defining event of UK women's hockey. Only two years before, we had come eleventh in the World Cup. We were ranked seventh in the world. We had beaten the Dutch previously but they were seen as the dominant, invincible force. Plus, the GB women's squad had never brought home a gold medal from an Olympic final.

Yet from the outset everything had clicked into place. Not long after we touched down in Brazil we found ourselves playing in perfect harmony. 'Shall we just call it a day now?' our coach Danny Kerry had joked after he blew the whistle on our first practice session. Normally in pre-tournament warm-ups, your body feels heavy and your lungs ache from the flight. Play feels stodgy and the ball clumsily pings off your stick as you try to trap it. Not this time. This time the ball moved smoothly. We moved smoothly. Something weird was in the air and we knew it. Danny knew it, too. We were a winning team before our gold medals were ever placed around our necks.

Fast-forward six years and I was sitting in the stands at Wembley waiting to watch the England Women's football team file on to the pitch. I'd travelled to see the Lionesses' final against

Germany in Euro 2022 with my friend Kirsty – a fellow Rio Olympics squad member and someone I'd known since we were teenagers, working our way up through the junior ranks in international hockey.

On the way there, we'd paused to take in the sweep of Wembley Way and watch the crowds swarming towards the stadium to the backdrop of car horns beeping and flags proudly displaying the St George's Cross.

'Can you believe it?' we said to one another. We knew the game was a sell-out – with England in the final it had become one of the hottest tickets in town – but there was something about being slap bang in the middle of it, noticing young girls smiling and laughing with their families and dressed in their England strips that stopped us in our tracks.

Once inside the stadium, that feeling only got stronger: 'Wow! All of these people are here to see women's football? Oh. My. God. This is amazing,' we said. In fact, the 87,000 fans poised to watch one of the most thrilling games of the season turned out to be the most to witness any men's or women's European Championship final in the UK's sporting history. As for the game itself, at times it left us both speechless. The entire tournament had already been marked out by its breathtaking quality of play, but this felt like women's football had reached another stratosphere. The Lionesses played with an effortlessness, confidence and freedom that reminded me of how we felt during our Rio final. Similarly, the match came down to the wire with forward Chloe Kelly stabbing home the final goal in the 110th minute in extra time. Everything clicked. It sounds cheesy, but it really is the stuff that dreams are made of.

For me, it was Chloe's winning-goal celebration that summed up everything, and not just for women's football, but for the whole of women's sport. As she turned and ran into the penalty area, she tore off her jersey to reveal her sports bra, swinging her strip around her head as she ran. One moment of unstoppable, irrepressible joy that got her a yellow card, but in my view it was a stroke of genius. I'd be surprised if there was a woman watching who didn't think, 'Go on, girl!' Overnight, it became the defining image of a new era. To me it said, 'I'm a woman. We're women doing great things and this is the female body achieving great things.'

Women's sport has never looked or felt so good as it does now, in 2023. In the past decade or so, individual successes and team victories have taken centre stage in ways I couldn't have imagined at the start of my career. Following the introduction of National Lottery funding for elite sport in 1997, the London 2012 Olympics saw a roster of women become household names. Heroines like heptathlete Jess Ennis-Hill, rower Katherine Grainger, boxer Nicola Adams and cyclist Laura Kenny were all elevated to gold-medal superstars. Two years later, England's triumph at the 2014 Rugby World Cup became a catalyst that has led to the Roses dominating the leaderboard in the Six Nations Championship. In tennis, the sight of an eighteen-year-old Emma Raducanu smashing it at the US Open in 2021 is another history-making moment imprinted on my brain – the line-up of stellar achievements is just too long to list here.

But the reality that women caught up in the sheer exhilaration of loving their sport has not always been embraced may surprise many of those young girls that Kirsty and I watched as we made our way down Wembley Way. Women's sport as we are enjoying it now is only the result of many, many women breaking down the barriers that have either prevented them from participating in sport or stopped them from being visible.

Sadly, history is littered with so many stories of women being banned from sports such as boxing, football or running, or having to meet in secret just to compete together. In the past, sport for women has been labelled unfeminine, socially unacceptable or too dangerous. I only need to look to my own sport – hockey. A match report from the first ever league game in 1890 says it all: 'When the teams took up their positions they made a pretty scene… the spectacle was quite animating, not to say charming.' Today, I dare any pundit to write that about the truly awe-inspiring women who have sweated, bled and beamed their way into the history books.

But while our changing landscape feels far more positive, some hangovers from that outdated era still exist. In 2022, the Northern Ireland women's football manager Kenny Shiels attributed his side's loss to women being 'more emotional' than men. In other words, women are still not seen as strong enough for the cut and thrust of competitive sport. Judging by archaic comments like that, we still have a long way to go.

There are other challenges, too. Fears that any gains made in achieving parity in women's sport may have been wiped out by the Covid-19 pandemic are real. Cancelled seasons for women's sports resumed long after men started playing again. Lack of access to training equipment and space to train during lockdowns also put a disproportionate number of women on the back foot, given that more female teams lack dedicated training facilities. And funding and sponsorship that existed pre-pandemic is not guaranteed going forward.

Elite sportswomen are also demanding more attention is given to issues that uniquely affect them. Many more now want to train and compete during pregnancy and after childbirth, yet only a handful of governing bodies have woken up to how this might be achievable. Scientific study around women's physiology is also only just scratching the surface about how periods or menopause can affect women athletes throughout their careers.

Debate about the inclusion of transgender athletes alongside balancing fairness and safety in sport for biologically female athletes is also a live issue. It's a conversation that has become polarized in the media, yet deserves open, nuanced and ongoing discussion. Like many of the female athletes I talk to, I want to guard against the risk of unfair advantage when it comes to athletic ability. However, I believe both inclusion and fairness at all levels of sport are possible.

Away from elite competition, participation of schoolgirls in sport remains significantly lower than that of boys. In so many of the schools I visit, girls tell me that being judged and lack of confidence are reasons why many lose interest in sport as they become teenagers. That sport is still not considered cool for girls is a real bugbear of mine, especially when there's so much raw talent out there turning outdated stereotypes on their head.

Girls being denied access to certain sports at school, such as contact games like rugby or football, is also holding us back. As I write, the UK government has pledged to make the same sports available to both boys and girls in schools, wherever wanted. It's an encouraging move and it will be interesting to see how much take-up there is. But a historic lack of visible female role models in those sports may also be another reason why progress has been slow. To me, it's not rocket science. After the Lionesses' Euro 2022 win and the coverage it received, there was a dramatic increase in sporty girls dreaming of their own successes in years to come. The phrase 'If you can't see it, you can't be it' has never rung so true. And role models aren't always found at the elite level. All of the amazing women interviewed for this book got inspired by teachers, family members, coaches or women they competed with in their local clubs. Participation and enjoyment always begin at the grassroots.

Thankfully, the appetite for watching women's sport is growing. In 2022, broadcast audiences doubled from 17 million the previous year to 36 million. Pre-pandemic levels were even higher. In 2019 an estimated 59 per cent of viewers had watched women's sport on three or more occasions compared to 57 per cent in 2022. A constantly improving standard of play, the knock-on effect of which is often increased viewing figures and growing sponsorship interest, is in part down to sustained investment and it's made women's sport more exciting than ever. That said, worldwide print and broadcast coverage still averages a pitiful 4 per cent.

Sponsorship deals are also improving but progress is slow. Similarly, the number of women moving into leadership positions in governing bodies and sports associations is increasing, but not fast enough. As for what we know about the journeys of many of Britain's sportswomen, there is still a frustrating lack of exposure. Mainstream sports media is awash with stories of men's sports. Fans know their favourite competitor's histories and the twists and turns of their careers. They root for their heroes because they feel they understand them and know their backstories.

The same cannot be said for most sporting women. Flick through the pages of most newspapers and you'll still find reports on how women look while they are playing sport, not their actual performance. As for women's stories, there are so many tales of bravery and determination, hardship and personal sacrifice. It's the reason why I wanted to put together this book. Most sports fans see and remember athletes clutching medals or trophies, laughing, crying or singing the national anthem. While those snapshots are a vital part of the experience for any athlete reaching the top of their game, success stories are never simply about those moments.

Behind every elite sportswoman's success or gut-wrenching loss is years of hard graft: there's the marginal gains built from season to season; the intense periods of self-doubt; the setbacks due to physical injury or mental health; the overwhelming pressure of being thrust into a media spotlight. Everyone has a compelling story to tell, and I believe it's more important than ever that women from many different backgrounds and with a variety of experiences share these stories to inspire every girl out there who may want to take up sport as a profession or as a lifelong hobby.

In sitting down with some of the most influential women in sport, I wanted to show elite sport's gritty reality alongside its triumphs. I've learned so much through these conversations. Javelin thrower Fatima Whitbread tells the story of how sport saved her from a devastating childhood. Marathon champion Paula Radcliffe sheds light on the agony of the long-distance runner. Hockey captain Kate Richardson-Walsh speaks about how coming out as gay informed her approach to leadership and building teams. Para-athlete Sarah Storey discusses balancing a medal-winning career with being a mum. And, my youngest interviewee skateboarder Sky Brown gave me so much hope for the future. Her mantra of 'girls can do anything' is infectious. Each one of the sportswomen featured here has helped women's sport evolve to where it is today.

I only have to look back at how I came to be on that podium in Rio in 2016 to understand how some of those personal battles and wider prejudices discussed in this book have affected me. My own passion for sport didn't begin in hockey at all, but in football. Growing up in the shadow of Liverpool Football

Club in the 1990s, I was handed my first Reds strip at the age of seven. That year, a 23-year-old Steve McManaman lifted the Football League Cup with two goals in the 2-1 win over Bolton at Wembley. Glued to the TV with my family, I was hooked.

Back then, footballing heroines didn't exist. Of course, they were out there and my interview in this book with the first ever England captain Sheila Parker was a truly humbling experience. But girls like me didn't know about women like Sheila and we certainly didn't see them on TV. Truly, I would have *loved* a Lioness to idolize. As for seeing role models who were mixed-race Chinese-British like me, that would have been off the scale. Instead, I had to make do with the lads catapulted from my home-town streets of Toxteth and Bootle into first-league legend.

I guess I was fortunate in that my twin brother Shaun shared my passion. We had goalposts set up in the garden and as I played with him and his mates I pretended to be 'Macca', shouting a running commentary as I raced down the wing: 'McManaman crosses for Fowler, who shoots and scores!' When I was nine, I started going with him to play for my local team, the West Kirby Panthers. The fact that it was a boys' league meant nothing to me. I played a couple of times in midfield and had the time of my life. But it wasn't long before I discovered that I wasn't welcomed by everyone.

When I showed up with my dad and joined in the pre-match practice, no one cared, but the minute I got my kit on ready to play, the comments started. From the sidelines I heard things like 'Oh my God, there's a girl playing football!' A few weeks went by before my mum got a message from the local FA saying that complaints had been made about a girl playing football. From then on I was banned from the children's league.

Naturally, my mum wasn't going to accept that and complained to the national FA, but by the time I was given a temporary reprieve until I reached eleven – at that time the age at which girls were allowed to play in boys' teams under official FA rules – it came too late in the season. Stubbornly, it didn't stop me turning up every week and warming up with the boys. But before each match I was forced to slide my tracksuit bottoms back on and watch from the sidelines with my dad. Even now, I remember that feeling of being gutted I was stopped from participating in a sport that I loved.

Eventually, I joined Tranmere Rovers girls' team, one of only two girls' teams in my area. By then I was also excelling at hockey. And like many of the women featured in this book, such as the swimmer Rebecca Adlington who as a kid just loved the water, my career did not start by my thinking it was going to be a career at all. I thrived at sport and I just wanted to play.

Why hockey? I got into it purely because during school lunchtimes there were clubs for all sorts of sports. Mum had always instilled in me the ethos that while winning in sport was the main goal, enjoying myself was just as important and when I tried hockey, I naturally slotted in. I began in centre midfield and loved the pivotal role of helping with defence and setting up attacks. By the age of fourteen, I was playing in the women's league, running practice alongside football plus juggling my studies.

But for every successful sportswoman, there are people who have spotted your potential often when you couldn't. These unsung heroines and heroes fill these pages. For ex-England rugby player Shaunagh Brown it was the teachers who told her she was special. For wheelchair athlete Tanni Grey-Thompson it was her first coach. For me, one was a PE teacher called Mrs Concannon. She took me aside when I was twelve and told me I could go places with my hockey but I needed to join a club. As an ex-Scottish hockey international, she had some good advice. She also directed me towards a club that was in the national league rather than one local to me. She saw a pathway into competition for me a good four years before I made the decision to quit football and concentrate on the game that would end up defining my life.

That sport was not cool for girls was also a constant theme when I was growing up. While I was fortunate to have teachers who understood the progress I was making and helped me balance sport with my studies, peer-group pressure made life more difficult. I was Sam the sports geek who couldn't hang out in town with my mates or stay out late at parties even when I wanted to. Aside from a handful of girlfriends whom I'm still in touch with today, kids at school didn't understand what I was doing or to what level. Shaunagh Brown and Sarah Storey also speak eloquently about being 'different' at school and having to navigate the bullies.

Playing in a team was also challenging at times. Although now I believe that sport is one of the best ways to break down any barriers, at football practice I was teased for being the only girl who attended a private school. 'Here's the posh girl,' some would say. At hockey, it was my mixed-race heritage that sometimes became the focus for ridicule. Yet when we were all on the pitch we had one goal: to win. Even if you are under-confident and shy, sport forces you to communicate and work together, to win together and to lose together – it's a crucial element of success that I also discuss with England hockey captain Kate Richardson-Walsh.

And let's not forget the uncontrollable nerves of turning up to a club or to trials or to your first international call-up to play with a team you've never met. Sprinter Christine Ohuruogu describes that experience perfectly, as do other women in this book who remember those nerve-wracking milestones like they were yesterday. I am no different.

Having trialled for the England Under-18s team, I performed well enough to play for the Under-21s, and it was off the back of that that I was first earmarked for the Women's GB team. Oh. My. God. That's when reality hit. Before training at the National Sports Centre in Bisham Abbey in Berkshire, after a three-hour journey, I could barely eat breakfast. Instead, I arrived one hour early and sat with my dad in the car park feeling waves of nausea washing over me. When I eventually entered as the newbie, I worried about everything: from what I was going to eat for lunch to how quickly I was going to put my kit on – never wanting to seem too keen. Then, of course, the question became how I was going to impress the coaches when everyone looked so much more experienced than me.

But for the nervous excitement and elation of every call-up there are as many crushing disappointments. Some are played out behind the scenes and some in the full glare of the international media. Second chances don't always arrive, but what I've found astonishing about all the women I've talked to has been their persistence, determination and unflinching self-discipline to go back and try again, even when failure has been so agonizing. Athletes such as rower Katherine Grainger, who lost out on gold by the finest of margins but came back to make history, have great stories to tell. Confidence and toughness are always learned along the way, but I, like so many others, understand what it's like to come back from the point of giving up.

That year for me was 2009. I had already been selected for the London 2012 Ambition Programme, which gave young hopefuls a taste of what an Olympics looked and felt like, but everyone knew that if you got picked it was almost guaranteed you were one of the top two in the talent coming through to be selected to go on to be in the London 2012 Olympic squad. Yet, for me, that didn't happen. It being a home Olympics just rubbed salt into the wound. On that day in 2009 when I found out I hadn't made the team, I spent the whole day buried under a duvet. The embarrassment was crippling. But it was a feeling I was to get used to. Not only did selection not happen for me then, it didn't happen for me seven consecutive times throughout my career. And what most people don't realize is that even in the face of failure, you still have to train with team members who are going to the Olympics or to other major championships. 'Why am I here? I'm not even a reserve!' I kept asking myself. By 2012 I knew I was good enough to be in the GB squad, so why couldn't I get selected? After one gruelling training session I remember breaking down in uncontrollable tears.

What keeps sportswomen going back? It's a question I've asked every woman, and the answers are different for every athlete. For example, long-distance runner Paula Radcliffe talks brilliantly about the need to keep racing, even when your body is screaming that you should give up. For me, it was pure stubbornness. I'd worked so hard that I wanted a shot at an Olympics. Every woman also has imprinted on her brain an image of an Olympic hero or heroine and mine was Kelly Holmes. Watching her eyes almost pop out of her head with shock at winning the dream double 800 and 1500 metres in Athens in 2004 was the one moment when I thought, 'Wow. That's exactly where I want to be.' Those images really matter. For Fatima Whitbread it took twelve years to win her first major title in the 1970s. Nowadays, an athlete's access to support and knowledge aided by technology means that that process is often speeded up. That said, it took me eight years to reach an Olympics. When I did, it was because I'd been through every emotion possible to believe that I still had what it took.

After years of setbacks I also needed confirmation from my coach Danny Kerry. In one rather heated showdown he let me know: 'Sam, I rate you as one of the best defenders. You are an integral part of this team,' he said. It's all I needed to know to propel me to the next level.

Yet periods of self-doubt can take athletes way off course. Skeleton champion Amy Williams and Rebecca Adlington open up in this book about how impostor syndrome plagued them during parts of their careers. Looking back on my own, I probably let it define me far more than it should have done. Yet it is all part of the roller coaster of elite competition. Even now I can suffer from agonizing self-doubt – when I stepped up to be the first woman captain of *Question of Sport*, or when I'm presenting live television programmes. It's learning how to push through it that counts.

And when my big moment came, I grasped it with both hands. This time, my mum had the champagne on ice, confident I would be successful. I was but team sport is never about one person. It's about everyone coming together to play at the top of their game. Yet that confidence and freedom that we played with and the Lionesses played with in Euro 2022 doesn't happen in that one moment. It's built over years.

Understanding your opponent is also key. Whether an athlete competes in an individual discipline or as part of a team, any psychological gains that can give you the advantage really matter. On the day we walked out on to that pitch for our final in Rio, a calmness and composure we had never felt before washed over every single woman in our team. We were there to do a job, and to win. But when we turned to face our Dutch rivals, they were banging their hockey sticks against the corrugated iron stadium wall. 'They're nervous,' we thought. No doubt, it gave us the winning edge.

And winning does matter. I think it's a word that British female athletes were maybe uncomfortable believing before London 2012, but a change in mindset has been pivotal to how women's sport has grown in confidence and quality over the past decade. Before Rio 2016 we became unashamed winners – a culture shift that felt unnatural and difficult but which was vital to our success. And let's face it, no one wants to watch a sport when the home team isn't pushing their way through to semi-finals and finals, or sportswomen aren't racing, throwing or skateboarding their way to podium places. Simply put: winners create winners.

Now I see that growing confidence everywhere I look in women's sport. Whether it's football, rugby, swimming or cycling. You name it, there's a raft of world-beating talent out there who will inspire a generation into the next Olympics and Paralympics, just like the women in this book have inspired me. Certainly I hope my own daughter Molly, who is two years old at the time of writing, will never have to go through the serious hard graft that women have endured simply to be accepted in sport, if it's a path she ever chooses.

Most of all, I see women becoming comfortable in their own skins playing sport, being competitive and wanting to reach the top of their game, whether that's at school, at club level or at national or international competition. That more of us can be role models for others fills me with so much hope. I love sport. I love hearing the stories of women in sport, and I hope you will find these conversations as interesting and poignant, uplifting and joyful as I did having them.

Sam Quek, September 2023

CHAPTER 1

Making History

Paula Radcliffe MBE

LONG-DISTANCE RUNNER

'I couldn't run because I was crying. I couldn't breathe properly, but I sat on a rock and thought, "I'm not carrying on like this. I think I can do it."'

Fifty-one years ago, six women staged a sit-down protest at the start of the New York Marathon. It was 1972 and the first year that women had been allowed to race in the event. Conventional wisdom until that point was that long-distance running wasn't just unfeminine but physically damaging to women, especially their reproductive health. Astonishing now that doctors claimed it could make a woman's uterus fall out. When the US's Amateur Athletic Union lifted its ban, it insisted on the women's race beginning ten minutes ahead of the men's.

But for female runners fighting for equality, its 'separate but equal' ruling was unacceptable. When the starting gun sounded, 'The Six Who Sat' waited out the imposed head start cross-legged on the tarmac clutching handwritten banners before running with the men.

For me, born sixteen years later, it's hard to imagine just how far the acceptance of women in sport has come. One of those six women, Nina Kuscsik, gave a flavour of that time in a recent interview recalling how if she ever trained on roads, police persistently pulled her over. 'They always assumed I was running away from something. It didn't cross their mind I could just be out running,' she told reporters.

And it's these steps that I also retrace with the legendary Paula Radcliffe when we speak. Her 2003 women's marathon record – a blistering 2 hours, 15 minutes and 25 seconds – remained unbroken for sixteen years. Now most major city marathons have reverted to staggered starts, but Paula – who has fought a fair few of her own sporting battles – tells me how important that legacy was in paving the way.

Now there are separate starts to showcase the women's event, and it's how the women's world record has evolved. It's not to belittle women or get them out of the way before the proper race comes. It's also to allow the media to show it properly and for people to watch it properly. It's for a different reason and it's a respectful reason.

What I hadn't appreciated is just how much Paula's own achievements are rooted in that same era – the 1970s and 1980s were *the* decades when women's long-distance icons emerged. She reels off names like Grete Waitz, who in 1979 became the first woman to run the New York Marathon in under two and a half hours; Joan Benoit Samuelson, who in 1984 became the first female marathon Olympic champion; and 1980s former world record holder Ingrid Kristiansen – one of the most formidable runners of her generation whom Paula, aged just twelve, came within touching distance of.

One of my earliest memories was meeting my dad at the London Marathon. We were waiting for him at different points to give him his mini Mars bar and carton of orange juice. It was 1985 and I saw Ingrid Kristiansen setting the world record. Then, the women ran with the men so she was among the top 100 men, but it felt like she was really close to the front. I was in awe of how quick she was running and how well she was running. She was so iconic wearing her trademark white gloves with her short hair and she ran in men's kit surrounded by TV cameras. Men ran with her just to be running with the leading female in the race. I remember thinking it was really cool that she was beating so many of them and she looked so strong. I was also captivated by the atmosphere of the marathon – it has an energy that if you are a runner you really pick up on. It inspired me.

But marathon runners like Paula aren't made, they're built. No one starts out fully formed or even necessarily wanting to run marathons. Instead athletes take incremental steps. Having been blessed with the perfect physique for her sport, Paula was first introduced to cross-country running, where many long-distance champions of both sexes have earned their stripes. A hearty breakfast of cheese and tomatoes on toast before getting filthy muddy are some of her fondest memories, but she also explains that cross-country taught her everything about her body's strengths and weaknesses and the tactics of the long-distance race.

I was lucky that I found the sport that I loved early on. From the beginning I enjoyed how running made me feel. There were times when I didn't want to train but I liked that battle between my body and my mind. And it's probably why I drifted towards marathon in the end because that's the ultimate challenge against your mind. I also felt really alive. When you're running fast and the wind is in your hair and the trees are going by it feels like all your senses are on alert.

Cross-country was the way I got started and it's brilliant. There's no clock so time doesn't matter, and you learn what type of course you run well on. You learn how to get a fast start which is really important. And it teaches you that fine line between the maximum effort you can sustain for the duration of the race and doing too much too soon. Too many athletes look at their heart rate, or look at their split times and that's not relevant in cross-country. You need to be looking at the course and where you are putting your feet. It stood me in really good stead for the marathon because you have to red-line it. You have to know what your body is capable of because if you go too fast you can't get over the finish. You run out of fuel.

I was also really lucky that when girls hit puberty their body shape can completely change, but mine didn't. My hips didn't grow massively. I didn't get boobs – not great for a teenager, but great for a runner.

That said, Paula may never have realized her potential had it not been for the support of her parents, especially her dad who had been a keen runner at school. Sadly, Peter passed away in 2020 but the way Paula describes him, he sounds like a legend. Just before she was born he took up marathon running to lose weight after giving up smoking. Living in Cheshire, the Mersey Marathon became a prominent date on the Radcliffe family calendar, as did the London Marathon. Later, in Paula's early teens when her parents relocated to Bedford, Peter spent time researching the best running club for Paula to join. That was Bedford and County Athletic Club where the coach Alex Stanton soon spotted her talent.

Dad used to drive us up to cross-country races in places like Durham back in the 1980s. He'd work all week and then get up at 5 a.m. on his weekends. It was a four- or five-hour drive with a car full of kids. We'd all race and then he'd drive us back again.

The cross-country courses were so muddy that he would tape our spikes up with masking tape. He'd tape round the bottom and over the laces and he'd be at the finish with his penknife cutting every shoe off. He said, 'If you are going to lose your shoe, can you at least remember what field it's in because I'd rather not walk around the whole course!'

And I can only remember him shouting at me once. I'd gone to run in Mansfield. It was what was called my first 'red vest' as I was representing the South of England against the North and the Midlands. I was so nervous and during the warm-up I walked over to Dad and said, 'I feel really sick.' He said to me, 'If you're not enjoying it, I'm not bringing you. It's meant to be fun. I don't care whether you come first or last, I just want you to enjoy it.' I didn't know it at the time, but years later I learned he'd stopped competing at school because he was being sick as he got so nervous. It was as if he'd come full circle.

Paula's coach Alex Stanton also placed an emphasis on Paula's enjoyment, in my view a message that's so important when you're starting out and even throughout your career. I recall during the 2012 Olympic cycle after I'd watched so many replays of me getting passes and dribbles wrong that I took all that negativity out on to the pitch. But in 2014 I worked with a sports psychologist who encouraged me to quit watching the tapes, to relax and enjoy my hockey. It was the key that unlocked everything, and I wondered whether Paula ever felt plagued by similar self-criticism and pressure?

Alex always said, 'You're never going to be an amazing under-15 or 16 or 17 because I want you to be a good senior. And he never increased the training by more than 10 per cent each year. I picked it up slowly. I wasn't training twice a day at that time so there was lots of space. He drilled that into me. And he also drilled into me that I needed to get my university degree. He said in sport you are always only one injury away from having to rely on that and my parents were keen I did too.

Plus, my dad always used to say, 'It is what it is. Make the most of it. You get what you are handed on the day.' It became a challenge to see what I could do on the day with the conditions I had. But you can't worry about it.

What's amazing to me is that it didn't occur to Paula that she could be a good runner until she was eighteen. That year she won the World Junior Cross Country Championships in Boston with a technique also taught to her by her dad. At the top of the hills when other competitors took a breather, she sprinted down knowing there would be a natural gap to catch her breath. And while her years at university also gave her a breather, they became a valuable transition period to build in track and road running, moving from 5000 metres to 10,000 metres distances and cementing the next stage of her career.

By today's standards Paula came to marathon running late. It wasn't until she was twenty-five that she won her first world half-marathon title and finally found her calling. It would be another two years before she debuted at the London Marathon in 2002. Then, as the UK's only female world-class distance runner, her nerves must have been in overdrive, but who can forget her characteristic head bobbing and her arms powering as she turned into the home straight. She didn't just end up winning, but set the women's world record (for the London course) and ran just shy of the overall women's world record.

It was a conscious decision not to run the marathon until then. All the physiologists I'd worked with said I was going to be better suited to it, but I wanted to be ready. It's hard, and I didn't want that first experience to put me off. My attitude was I had nothing to lose. If I screwed up it was because it was my first one. But at the same time, I wanted to prepare really well and just go and enjoy it.

We didn't have a time in mind at all, but Alex said, 'Just go out and have fun. I'm not going to tell you to make any moves, just have fun.' But when I went to the loo beforehand people kept coming up and telling me how much money they'd bet on me. I didn't want to know because I felt too much pressure, but the support was something unreal. And when you're out there and leading it, it's just mental.

I got away around the Cutty Sark *without even trying to. The crowd was so thick but I must have picked up the pace. When I looked around I thought, 'Shit, there's no women!' But Dad used to say, 'Do not look behind. Either you are going to look stupid and fall flat on your face or you are going to tell people behind that you're worried about them.' After that I*

didn't look. I had no clue how far I was ahead. I had no clue
until I turned on to The Mall and I saw the big clock and it said
2.18. I thought, 'Shit! The world record is 2.18!' but I didn't
have time to make it up. I missed it by nine seconds, but when
I crossed the line I said, 'I can definitely get that.'

If Paula's marathon debut isn't proof enough that women are
built for endurance running, then the science is now also chipping
away at outdated wisdom. Remarkably, early evidence suggests
exactly the opposite of the previous theory. Women have been
found to pick up speed over longer distances, narrowing the
gap between them and their male counterparts. Over very long
distances, like ultra-marathons which can run to 200 miles,
they outperform men on a minute-per-mile basis. The reasons
are yet to be fully discovered, but the answer may lie in the
female hormone oestrogen, which allows our bodies to burn
more fat. Differences between male and female muscle fibres
may also hold a clue.

The physiotherapist Gerard Hartmann, who worked with
Paula for fourteen years from 1997, described her not as a
natural thoroughbred, but someone who had to work hard
at being the best. Her real super-power, he said, lay in her
ability to endure more pain than anyone he'd ever seen. Her
extraordinary tenacity, focus and meticulous preparation also
allowed her team to transform her from an excellent athlete
into an all-time great.

By then that team consisted of a raft of dedicated professionals including her husband Gary, who gradually took over as her coach from Alex Stanton from around 2003. Although Alex remained central to Paula's training throughout her entire career, it was Gary who picked up the reins as Alex's eyes on the ground as Alex began to travel less in later years. Given Gerard's description, I was fascinated to know how Paula developed that physical toughness and how she stopped the mind gremlins from biting over a course of twenty-six miles?

I think I was naturally quite good at tuning pain out. I have a high threshold. It wasn't as if I was being brave. I'd do silly things like run to the track with my spikes on my back, do the session, run home, get into the shower, and then I'd realize the spikes had cut through my back and I hadn't even felt it. I also liked the challenge of trying to block it out and trying to focus only on what's important and not the rest.

One of the things that I learned in cross-country training was that to pass the time I started counting. With Alex, I used to do four six-and-a-half-minute reps, and those increased to five reps as I got older. But I'd play this little game to try and work out where I was. Alex would blow the whistle at three minutes and with a minute to go, then thirty seconds to go so I started trying to guess when he was going to blow the whistle. In the marathon, that was useful because the whistle blew at five minutes which was pretty much a mile, so I could guess and know it's where I wanted to be. I thought, 'This is great, it passes the time, and I can work out when the mile marker is coming up.'

And when that does help is when you are going through a rough patch. On a good day there may be a couple. It just feels harder. Your breathing is a little bit harder and you notice blisters, or you need the loo or you notice you have a tummy ache or a stitch, or little things like something rubbing and you can't stop to do something about it. To focus on something as simple as counting shuts all those off.

Later, in 2002, when Paula went on to compete in the Chicago Marathon, she powered through some of those problems that may have wobbled others. As an asthma sufferer from childhood, she developed bronchitis following London and missed a chunk of training. Then, just before she was due to compete on the track in the run-up she developed a blister.

I'd started my track season late and when I got this really bad blister I was in Limerick. Gerard told me I basically had to piss on it. I had to pee and let the open wound on the arch of my foot soak it up, so I sat there with a cup of urine and a cotton wool pad. It dried out the skin. After that I learned there's a spray dog owners use to harden a dog's feet, so I used that if I had a blister. Just after, I went into the Monaco Diamond League and ran a personal best, and another personal best at the Commonwealth Games in Manchester.

But as the Chicago Marathon drew closer, it was Paula's menstrual cycle that threatened to destabilize her race. It's every sportswoman's fear, and thankfully more of us are talking about how menstruation affects our performance. Again, research is in the early stages, and Paula agrees more is needed, but for athletes who suffer extreme symptoms it can be the difference between finishing first or last. Besides, high-intensity exercise at certain times of our cycles can lead to injury as our ligaments can sometimes be weaker. Nowadays, athletes are often asked to record their monthly cycles during training and competitions, but in Paula's era the subject was definitely taboo and she was left to her own guesswork.

My periods didn't really affect me, but you still don't want to have one on race day. Many years before, British Athletics had put me in touch with a doctor as I was only getting two or three periods a year. He said it was going to affect my bone density so they put me on the pill.

I remember racing at Crystal Palace not long after, and it was the trials for the World Championships. Suddenly, I started feeling dizzy walking up and down the steps, and I began spotting in the warm-up. It really stressed me out because I wasn't due. One of the ladies gave me a tampon and told me to put it out of my mind and race. I went out and came fourth, but it was the first three girls who qualified.

At the time my agent was a guy called Andy Norman who was known as a bit of a bully but actually he was a softie at heart. After the race I'd been up all night crying and he called me and said, 'You're on a plane to Oslo next week and in two weeks you are racing the girl who came third. You'd better fucking win.' I went to see my doctor, came off the pill, went to Oslo, raced a personal best and came back and beat the girl.

It did all work out, but I was wary of going near the pill after that. However, I did end up taking it for short amounts of time to move my period away from major championships. But I screwed up in Chicago. I should have had my period the week before but it was late. I wanted it to come so badly because I always felt worse a couple of days before with bloating and heavy legs. But it came that morning. I thought, I'm just going to have to make the best of it. I had really bad stomach cramps but not until around the 22-mile mark so I knew I could have run faster.

That Paula says she should have run faster blows me away considering she ended up smashing her previous best time set in London that April. By running the course in 2 hours, 17 minutes and 18 seconds she beat the world record set by the mighty Catherine Ndereba the previous year *and* demolished her heroine Joan Benoit Samuelson's 1985 Chicago time by four minutes. How did she feel in that moment?

It's quite surreal. You think it's going to be bigger than it is. You finish and you are freaking knackered. Everything hurts and you can barely walk. Then you get pulled into press, then you have to go to doping control. When the woman came out and shouted 'next' I said, 'I'm really sorry I have to change a

tampon!' I couldn't do that without going to the loo so I got
to jump the queue.

An hour later I was sitting in an ice bath with Gary banging
on the door saying that I had to hurry up to go to the sponsors'
reception. I thought, 'Seriously? I've just run a world record and
I have to go shivering upstairs to say hi to the sponsors!' So it's
funny, because you think it's going to be something amazing,
and it is amazing. But I wasn't jumping up and down because
I had no energy. Instead of it being a massive high, it's more
like a quiet satisfaction. I felt more complete, a bit like I did
after childbirth.

But I was really pleased my time was 2.17. My grandma
was born on 17 December. She was born prematurely and not
expected to live, but she died aged ninety-six. She got married
on the 17th, my dad was born on the 17th and my daughter
was born on the 17th. And when I competed for Bedford at
English Schools XC, I was always number seventeen.

Over the next three years, Paula was catapulted into being a
household name, bringing with it a press intrusion she now
admits completely overwhelmed her and prompted her eventual
relocation to Monaco. But she was also to experience the most
dramatic highs and lows of her entire career, making her dad's
wisdom of 'making the most of the day' more meaningful. As
she pushed on with an ambition to smash her Chicago record
the following year in London 2003, a more serious disaster
almost stopped her.

I was in Albuquerque running on the Rio Grande. Gary was alongside on the bike. We did the same course each week, and each week we would try to go further. I was in the last mile, trying to push on and this little kid was on her bike. As I ran round past her she looked behind to see where her mum was and as she turned her head she turned the wheel. It caught my back foot and I face-planted on to the path at 19km an hour. I was so tired, I didn't have time to put my hands out. I had so many cuts and scrapes and I'd smashed my heart rate monitor. Gary was freaking out. He was screaming at the woman, and she was terrified she'd get sued as we were in America.

There's a picture taken of me when we got to the physio and it looks like I'm dead. It wasn't all right because I had whiplash. I tried to run the next day, but couldn't. I was like a stone. I couldn't even jog for twenty minutes. After about a week, the worst thing was the road burn blisters on my shoulders which I put Compeed on but it kept peeling back when I ran. My hip was also jammed. I must have compacted it in some way so I was worried going into London. My physio was treating it every day but warned me before the race that it was going to lock up and get sore but probably towards the end.

Then, three days before London we got a call to say the guy who had driven us home from a press conference had gone down with bad gastric flu. Just as we were arriving into London, Gary started throwing up. We put him in a different room in the hotel and he wouldn't even come out. He would only talk to me through the door or on the phone. Thank God I never got it.

When I opened the curtains on race day it was all absolutely fine and the weather looked good. And there was the biggest pop out of my hip in the last pre-race massage. I thought, that's a good sign. All of these things that could have gone really badly wrong didn't, so I wanted to make the most of it.

But making the most of it also took tremendous planning. Race director Dave Bedford and Paula's team had another world record in their sights, but he didn't feel Paula could do it without the use of male pacemakers – a controversial move in the run-up. In a women-only race some rival athletes claimed it would give Paula an unfair advantage, and that the race should remain an all-women race run with female pacemakers. Pacemakers not only provide a target to aim for but shield runners from headwinds, and male pacemakers maintain a higher pace and can run longer into a race. Athletics' governing body, the IAAF, also raised an eyebrow. In the end, a compromise was struck: the pacemakers would run to the finish, effectively making it a mixed race.

Dave didn't believe I could break the record without the pacemakers. He was blunt about it. I thought I could, but he said, 'I'm not taking that risk. If it's a windy day, I want a couple of guys so you can shelter from the wind.' I wasn't going to make a massive fuss. By that point, they'd checked it was legal but I said, 'Just be aware that I'm going to run alongside them because I don't want people to think I sheltered behind them all the way.'

It's true that a lot of runners do find it hard to push themselves on their own, but I always felt I could push myself harder. At the time, the women's world record was my record, so I decided I was just going to run it like I was racing the men. One of them dropped out somewhere around the 17-mile mark, so that was him beaten. I just had to beat the other one.

When I came into the home straight there was a lovely guy called Harry Fry who worked on the marathon team jumping up and down and cheering me on. He was later reprimanded for being too enthusiastic, but it was the best thing I could see. He sent the pacemaker one way and me the other. It's the same distance, but he got a second quicker so I was pissed off I didn't beat that one. But I was really hurting. My stomach was a mess. Your colon bounces up and down when you run and I'd taken the lining off the inside of my colon. It was bleeding and I felt like I was going to throw up.

Gary doesn't have much of a filter. He went over to my mum and said, 'Have you got some make-up because she looks like shit!?' My mum got so defensive. 'Don't speak about my daughter like that!' she told him.

Fast-forward eight years and it was Paula's almost unimaginable world record from that day of 2 hours, 15 minutes and 25 seconds that was to come under threat. In 2011 the IAAF ruled to retrospectively downgrade her performance to a world best. Her use of pacemakers, it decided, meant her record was achieved in mixed conditions. Only times secured in all-women competitions would be acknowledged for world-record purposes.

Outrageous in my view, but Paula downplays it saying doping allegations levelled at her four years later, of which she was cleared, felt far more damaging to her mental health and her reputation. That said, she made her protest clear as did many of her supporters, eventually forcing an IAAF climbdown.

I thought, screw you. You can try. I ran it. It felt very petty. I was living in Monaco by then so I went to see Lamine Diack who was head of the IAAF. He was running it to rack and ruin and it was extremely corrupt. He was in his slippers in his penthouse and he hadn't a clue about the decision. I said to him, 'You were in the meeting!' He said, yes, but he'd fallen asleep. He was actually asleep when that rule was voted on. It was a predominantly male council plus a male president who was asleep. They'd voted on a rule without asking any of us to speak beforehand. But I had a huge amount of support. Nike put out a T-shirt with the words 'History Stands' on it.

Yet the one achievement that did truly escape Paula was to win an Olympic gold medal at Athens 2004. Watching the footage back now, it feels utterly heartbreaking. Twenty-two miles in and she was forced to stop, tears pouring down her cheeks and her distress palpable. While medics believed she may have had heatstroke, they later put it down to the side effects of the anti-inflammatory drugs she'd taken to relieve the pain of a huge bruise underneath her thigh muscle, probably combined with stress. In the run-up she hadn't been absorbing food properly, and as she ran her stomach began to cramp violently. Barely able to put one foot in front of the other, her body effectively shut down and hit the marathon wall of running out of fuel. I know that every fibre of her being would have been screaming, 'Carry on!' How hard was it to put her own health first?

On a scale of one to ten, London was five in discomfort, but in Athens I knew I could carry on a bit further but I was not going to finish that race. I couldn't run in a straight line and I kept edging back to the gutter. I thought, this is actually going to destroy me but I'm going to stop. It was really hard. I stopped once and started again, but I had to stop.

Afterwards the media came out and called me a quitter and I started to think, 'Well maybe I could have carried on?' It played over and over in my mind. But Rob de Castella, who'd been a massive icon in marathon running, wrote to me saying that I would look back on it and be glad. My body did listen when it needed to. He told me his didn't and he ran into heat exhaustion. He said he ended up on a drip and was never the same afterwards.

The Olympics is still not my favourite event, and it felt really unfair that it never worked out. But there are lots of areas in my life where things did work out. I'm naturally a person who looks on the bright side. For me it was much easier than for my husband. Gary has really struggled with it. He knew that on any other day I would have been all right. And because I was the one out there, there was nothing he could do. He didn't talk about it, whereas I did and I let all my emotions out and cried for a long time. I worked through it but he still feels bitter and pissed off.

What surprises me is that Paula had the balls to go out five days later to run the 10,000 metres even though she was clearly unwell, and in the end couldn't finish. Still not 100 per cent, she then announced she would compete in the New York Marathon later that year. Why?

I wanted to know if I could salvage anything. I needed to find the answer, and the answer in the 10k was that I had to step off. At that time, I didn't know how big it was at home, that I was being called a quitter. My phone had been going mental but I hadn't been looking at it. I only knew my emotions.

When it came to New York, I made that decision after I'd gone away to train. We'd never had the paparazzi outside the house before, but now they were hiding in bushes. They even rang my doctor's surgery and asked for the results of a pregnancy test that didn't exist because someone had told them that's what could have been wrong with me. It was really freaky.

So we went to Flagstaff and I had this epiphany moment. I'd read a piece by the table tennis player Matthew Syed about how I was a quitter and how I only ever ran for money which was so untrue. I was in the foothills and I couldn't run because I was crying. I couldn't breathe properly, and I sat on a rock and thought, 'No, I am not going to let them take something I love doing so much away from me. I'm not carrying on like this.' After one long run a week or so later, I said to Gary, 'I think I can do it. I want to race again.'

It was only a few days before the marathon when I went into the press conference that it hit me that the whole of the media reckoned it was going to be a car crash. I was a basket case. I thought, 'This is shit. They all think I can't do this.' But for me it didn't matter. So long as I was healthy and I could finish a race then it didn't bother me. But winning is one of the reasons I love New York. After Athens I could get to New York. It worked out.

These days Paula runs for fun as well as encouraging kids and families to run for enjoyment too. In Monaco she's less Paula Radcliffe and more mum to her daughter Isla and son Raphael. That she inspired a whole generation of girls makes her smile, but she also appreciates how history evolves.

She was there on the finish line in Chicago, one of the first to congratulate a 25-year-old Brigid Kosgei in 2019 as she eclipsed her 2003 London Marathon time by 1.21 minutes – until then it had been the longest-standing marathon world record by a man or a woman since the Second World War. How hard was that for Paula knowing it was the end of an era?

I worried about how I was going to feel. I was in the VIP tent in Chicago and I could feel people looking at me and thinking, is she going to crack up? We thought Brigid was going to run out of fuel, but at 25km she got quicker. At that point we knew the record was going to go. Dave Bedford, who had held the world record for the 10,000 metres back in the early seventies, came over and said, 'You know, Paula. You're not going to change colour. You're going to be exactly the same person. You're just not going to be the world record holder any more.' It was a really nice thing to say, and he was right.

When I went out to meet Brigid, I'm not entirely sure she knew who I was as she was fatigued, and in that moment lots of things get thrown at you. Seeing her brought back memories of wanting time to celebrate, but you don't get that time. I knew she wouldn't have a moment to enjoy it, but that she'd just done something amazing. Afterwards I was handing out finisher medals to the masses for a couple of hours and it was surreal because many of the finishers didn't know the elite result so were asking me. I was informing them of my own record being broken. It felt a bit weird but also cathartic and helped me to push through my emotions faster. I then called my kids and realized that, of course, all the things that really mattered were exactly the same. When I got the world record I probably never expected to hold it for seventeen years. You have to accept that history moves forward.

CHAPTER 2

Into the Unknown

Amy Williams MBE

SKELETON RACER

'After that first try I just wanted to keep going. I didn't want to be seen as this weedy little girl doing skeleton and crying.'

Amy Williams wished she'd owned a camera phone when she began competing on the ice track back in 2002. If she had, she would have recorded more of her winning moments. For every athlete, they go by in a blur. But, she tells me, she also regrets not documenting the sheer agony of perfecting the art of skeleton racing.

As girls we were smaller and we could tuck ourselves into our sled a bit, but if you hit the walls hard your whole body thumped off the ice. We'd train with a camping mat stuck down us and Tubigrip taped to our elbows and ankles, but even then our ankles would get blown up black and blue. You could go to bed and the pressure from the G-force on your neck from a day's training meant you couldn't lift your head off the pillow the next day. You woke up aching from head to toe.

Death-defying ice sports like skeleton (head first, flat on your stomach), luge (feet first, flat on your back) and bobsleigh (seated in a high-sided sled) have always amazed me and terrified me, but I guess it wasn't until Amy claimed gold in the 2010 Vancouver Olympics that I fully bought into winter sports. I would have been in my late teens, getting serious about my hockey, when a 27-year-old Amy completed her final slide, fell into the arms of her coach and looked gobsmacked as she draped a GB flag around her shoulders.

Today, fans of ice sports might be more familiar with Olympian Lizzy Yarnold who won double gold in the skeleton in Sochi in 2014 and PyeongChang in 2018. Or bronze medallist Laura Deas who finished behind Yarnold in 2018. But for me, it is Amy who was the first queen of the ice. She had the look of the girl next door, and I loved every second of her hurtling head first at 90 mph on what looked like a tea tray straight into the history books.

That day, I was petrified at the top. My legs were shaking. I knew I was in gold medal position and that final run was either going to make me win or not. And when I got to the bottom and smashed into the foam, everyone was cheering. I thought, 'Are they cheering for me?' I asked my coach, 'Where did I come?' 'You're Olympic champion,' he told me. I couldn't even get my helmet off, and then someone from the crowd handed me a Union Jack flag which I couldn't unfurl properly. People were going crazy. When I look back at the footage now I think, is that me? Am I that girl?

The emotion of that moment isn't anything any athlete can prepare for, but Amy's win was monumental for so many reasons. At the end of the two-day competition in the last run, it took fifty-four seconds of her swerving corners and ricocheting off ice to become the first British woman in an individual winter event to win gold for fifty-eight years. And what's more surprising is that when Amy started out, ice sports weren't on her radar at all.

I loved sport and I joined an athletics club around the age of thirteen where I'd be on a Tuesday and Thursday night. For me, athletics was it. It was my love. And Bath Athletic Club was a community club. There was no expense, really. We got dropped off by our parents for an hour. We might have to buy a pair of spikes and at weekends we'd jump in with our coach and travel to Birmingham or whatever place was holding competitions. It was old-school.

Amy describes her upbringing near Bath as 'outdoorsy' but neither of her parents came from a sporting background and no one, including her twin sister and older brother, went on to pursue sport. Yet she talks fondly about her active childhood and believes it made her the person she is today.

My parents didn't have a TV in the house until I was around sixteen; we didn't have the money. Play was old-school too: you drew, you read, you occupied yourself. Our garden was surrounded by fields and countryside and Mum had a little bell to call us in. On Sundays we'd go to church, have lunch and Dad would always have planned a walk. It could be one hour or three hours. You never knew. And our holidays were spent youth hostelling around places like Devon – paying 50p to stay in a cow shed and cooking boil-in-the-bag rice and crabbing in the sea.

Like many of us, Amy isn't sure where her competitive streak comes from, but I recognize immediately her drive to challenge herself. For me, that drive was probably a stubborn desire to secure my place on a team and beat other girls eager to knock me off my spot. But every athlete is unique, and for individual competitors the motivation to keep going can be different.

I was a bit of a pleaser. I always wanted to do well and please my coaches. And then there was my internal voice asking, how fast can I run? If I complete all my training sessions, how much quicker can I make my time? In athletics it's so clear-cut. You run a race. You get a time. You train. You run another race and you see if your time gets faster. I loved seeing how much better I could become, and how much better I could make my body.

What astonishes me about Amy is not only how much better she wanted to make her body, but what she was prepared to put her body through from a very young age. As she continued running she excelled at 400 metres, but became plagued by shin splints – the debilitating ache runners often get across their shin bones. Back then, there was little knowledge about how pounding a pavement day in, day out might affect a runner, and Amy describes having to strap up her shins to relieve the pain just so she could sit her school exams. She faced operations where incisions would have to be made to the tissue around her leg muscles. In the end, she was forced to make the difficult decision not to continue.

I remember someone saying to me that I needed to do something else other than 400 metres because I was in so much pain. I was good, and I'd represented my county. But I hadn't got into the English Schools Athletics Championships or got to represent England so I knew I wasn't good enough. After school I went to art college in Bath and bumped into some people in the gym from Bath Athletic who were doing skeleton and bobsleigh. I loved training and I just wanted to be good at something, so I went out with them on the push track that had just opened at Bath.

*Modern pentathlon was also based at Bath University, so
I began fencing and shooting and horse riding too, which I'd
done growing up. It was 2002 and pentathlete Stephanie Cook
had not long since won gold at the 2000 Sydney Olympics.
Modern pentathlon also had funding and offered me a place,
but by that time I'd tried skeleton and been out on the ice.*

Before I spoke to Amy, I hadn't appreciated that, unlike many
foreign rivals competing in ice sports, bobsleigh and skeleton
hopefuls in the UK have no actual ice to train on. At Bath
University, the 140-metre push track was officially opened in
2002, the year of the Winter Olympics in Salt Lake City, and to
this day, it's the only place where UK athletes can practise. But
instead of sliding on ice, bobsleighs and sleds are built with four
wheels and slotted into a set of tracks, with a bungee system
to pull them back. A great starting ground, explains Amy, but
nothing in comparison to getting out on the frozen track where
wheels are replaced with runners that sit on the ice.

*When you finally get out on ice you have a different type of
sled than on the push track. It slips around and there's not the
same friction. And there's a whole mix of emotions that first
time. You're excited and nervous and scared. The adrenaline is
pumping because you're entering into a total unknown when
someone pushes you off. You start on the last six corners of the
track then on your next run you go up another two corners.
The second time is even scarier than the first. You know the*

first time you hit every wall and it really hurt. But the day you don't hit that same wall, it feels great. Suddenly you want to go down more and more without falling off or hurting yourself.

The lengths Amy went to in order to get out on the ice also speaks volumes about her determination. With the encouragement of a performance director at Bath she paid her own way to get to the World Push Championships in Groningen in the Netherlands in 2002. There, she surprised herself by coming second in the overall competition and also winning in the guest category, prompting people around her to suggest she travel to Norway to try the ice proper.

At that time, I was still in this predicament of wondering whether to pursue modern pentathlon. The sport had some amazing girls who were very, very strong and I knew there was Lottery funding available. But after doing so well in the Push Championships, I was asked if I'd go to Norway to try the ice in a military camp. It was around £2,500 to get there to train and I had to pay my own way. I didn't have that money and in the end my student loan paid for those two weeks. I remember only four civilians in the camp. It was mainly big marines and beefy bobsleigh army girls, but after that first try I just wanted to keep going. I didn't want to be seen as this weedy little girl doing skeleton and crying. It was two weeks of being beaten up but I loved it. Then, I had another thought: there were already a good bunch of girls doing pentathlon, so if I ever wanted

*to represent Great Britain I could do that much quicker if I
pursued skeleton. Far fewer women were doing it, so if I went
down that route, I knew I could compete.*

That few women were competing in skeleton at the time comes
as little surprise when you look at the patchy history of the
sport. While there's no record of women ever being banned
from taking part, there is also no official record of women ever
competing in the UK until the late 1990s when Alex Coomber
won the World Cup three years in a row from 1999/2000 to
2001/02.

At Olympic level, skeleton only ever appeared as a discipline
called Cresta in 1928 and 1948, and then only for men. For
women, it was considered too risky. For the next fifty-four
years it was removed from the Olympic programme altogether
because, unlike in 1928 and 1948, when both competitions
took place in St Moritz in Switzerland when there was a natural
bobsleigh track, artificial tracks weren't invented until much
later, prompting a rise in the popularity of the sport. Both
women and men were allowed to compete for the first time
in 2002 when the discipline was reintroduced to the Olympic
line-up and since then UK women have outperformed all other
nations.

Alongside Amy and Lizzy Yarnold clinching golds, Shelley
Rudman – Amy's main rival – took silver in Turin in 2006.
Alex Coomber was the first woman to win bronze in 2002 –
amazingly competing while nursing a broken wrist – followed

by Laura Deas seventeen years later. By comparison, the men's discipline has floundered, with only Dominic Parsons winning bronze in 2018. The Beijing Olympics in 2022 is the only year the British team have returned empty-handed in the men's and women's races. Given those statistics, I was interested to know how British women have consistently smashed it in the discipline when there's no snow or ice track to practise on and access to tracks worldwide is limited. Plus, every track is unique with different speeds and contours.

It's a bit like Formula One. All tracks have left and right turns but they are all very different, right down to every single corner. Some have big round circles and some half circles. Some are big G-force tracks with big, big corners. We call the gliding tracks low G-force tracks and they're slower – the kind of track where your shopping list might pop into your head when you're halfway down. For these you need tiny, fine movements on the sled to steer. Others you boom into really high G-force and you can crash and flip a corner. Then there are different types of ice: sticky, wet, frosty. The time of day will also affect the ice. Every track has its own little world around it, so whenever and wherever in the world we slide, we walk the tracks, make notes, look at each profile and we'd learn the key corners because, unlike the locals who have hundreds of runs, we have six runs to get it right.

All the time you are seeing how you can get speed out of every corner. You work with the highs and the lows and the oscillations, making sure your sled is at the correct angle to get that fastest route. And when we write notes we are also analysing our movements. If I dropped a toe on the way out to try and change the angle, did it work? Did it not work? What was the knock-on effect into the next corner?

That obsessive preparation is part of every elite sport, but the trick in skeleton is to pick up as much speed as possible across the 65-metre start using strength and power. When the clock starts at the 15-metre mark, the athlete prepares to leap on to begin the run. With no brakes or steering, they must change movement and speed with touches of their feet, or by manoeuvring their shoulders and legs, negotiating each twist and turn as they hit a G-force often five times the force of gravity, their faces centimetres from the ice. But it's not just intense physical preparation that matters, as Amy learned to her cost when she failed to qualify for the 2006 Turin Olympics. That year, she travelled as a reserve and it was her UK rival Shelley Rudman who took silver. When Amy reflects on that period, she believes she became consumed by a toxic atmosphere in the camp rather than focusing on her performance. The game-changer, she says, happened in the year's run-up to Vancouver when Amy was given access to a sports psychologist who shifted her mindset and turned her performance around.

Turin was a big turning point for me. It made me think, 'I'm never going to miss out on an Olympics again.' It put fire in my belly, but I wasn't the most confident person and with hindsight, I focused too much on the other girls. There was a horrible atmosphere in the camp and I was consumed. I nearly quit around 2005. I found the bitchiness so hard, and not having friends. You travel as a team, you share rooms, and you are expected to sit down and have dinner together, but you're competitors. When you stand on that start line you're not a team.

I've heard Lizzy Yarnold and Laura Deas say they were genuinely friends and I think how lucky they were. I think that's why they were more successful, but in my era it was really, really tough. No one helped you. They didn't want you to win. There were teammates who couldn't even say 'Good morning'. It was icy cold. In the end, my closest friends became the other nations. I would sit with the Aussies, the Germans, the Americans and the Canadians, and many are still friends to this day. I cried a lot in those years. You're away from home on six, seven or eight week blocks and you had your scratch phone cards with a minute to speak to your mum, and I spent half of that time crying.

And when it came to the track, I was even concentrating on other nations and what they were doing that I was not. I kept asking, 'Why are they faster? How come I'm not as good as them?' After Turin I knew I had four years to get to Vancouver, and I actually found confidence by having a tick-box focus on myself. I'd eaten the best, slept the best, prepared the best and trained the best. I started living my life every single day asking, 'Is this going to help me become a better athlete? Yes or no?'

The sports psychologist helped me focus on my performance and she also became a mediator between me and my coach to help that relationship become more trusting.

While Amy had several coaches over the years, her primary coach was former luge and skeleton racer Austrian Michael Grünberger, a person whom Amy has described in previous interviews as 'harsh, unemotional and old-school'. The language barrier didn't help either, she tells me, but when it comes to high-adrenaline sports, when you put your life in someone else's hands, isn't trust everything?

When it came to the physical slides, I trusted my coach completely. Even when it got to the Olympics I didn't watch any of the other videos of any of the other girls. I trusted him 100 per cent to tell me how I needed to improve or if I needed to steer differently. But it's a relationship, and you have good times and bad times. Sometimes you hate each other and sometimes you like each other but having a psychologist there gave me a sounding board and it helped me, and it helped him, and that relationship improved. I realized that I only performed well when I was happy. It was simple. And I was never happy on race days because of the pressure. My coach dubbed me 'training champion'. It's what he called me. I broke all track records in training, but never on race days. So, when it came to Vancouver and my preparation, he didn't understand what I wanted to achieve.

Over the previous year I'd figured out that on those training days, I was in my happy bubble. There were lots more distractions. You might be mixed in with the bobsleigh guys in this little changing room, so you've got things going on. Then, you walk out, put your helmet on, and you're focused on the slide. But on competition days it's deadly silent. No one talks. It's a completely different atmosphere.

So at the Vancouver Olympics I planned every second of that race from the moment I woke up. I took myself off to a different level of the building than the changing room. I taped up the windows with a Union Jack flag so I couldn't see the crowds outside. My physio was there, and a Czech bobsleigh guy I was dating at the time, and we created this happy bubble. It was as if I wasn't actually doing an Olympic race. We just sat around and chinwagged and recreated that training environment on race day. My coach accused me of not concentrating. He didn't quite get it until afterwards when he said, 'Ah, I see what you were doing there.'

I know exactly how hard it is to control nerves at those moments when it really counts, and it took me around five or six years of playing hockey internationally to get into the mindset of knowing that even if I made one mistake followed by another, I could pull myself back from the brink of self-doubt and stop it spiralling out of control. For Amy to develop that focus so quickly is admirable, especially because in Vancouver, only two days before she was due to compete, Georgian luge champion

Nodar Kumaritashvili died after losing control of his sled and hitting an unpadded steel pole in training. Amy recalls the shock waves it sent through the sliding community but her mental training kicked in. She told herself that the death happened on a different day and in a different discipline. It didn't mean she would die too. Instead, her thought process shifted to having utmost respect for the track.

But the intense pressure on Amy didn't just come from the competition itself. Despite her never having won a World Cup before and reaching silver in a World Championship the previous year, it became increasingly clear that Amy was the UK's main winning hope. As the competition progressed, rival Shelley Rudman recorded her two quickest slides, but could only reach sixth. At that time funding was allocated on four-year cycles and was based on medal potential, putting immense pressure on athletes to achieve, especially emerging talent in less represented sports. (The funding formula changed in 2020 to allocation based on medal potential over a twelve-year period.) Amy knew that if she won, it wouldn't just cement her own success, but also secure funding for the women's sport overall.

The biggest pressure is the pressure you put on yourself. I knew I'd won silver in Lake Placid the year before and I had to get a medal for myself. But I also knew I needed to get a medal for our team. You've got the pressure of the competition, the pressure of dealing with the coach, and you're also fighting because you know that if the sport doesn't receive the same money then it can't produce medals, because there isn't the funding to do the things you need to do. But, the work I did with the psychologist helped because I also learned to put that in a box and compartmentalize. Knowing that I needed a medal for the team wasn't going to make me slide any quicker. I could only control the controllables. I got into a way of thinking, 'If I do everything consistently, every single day, like I've done every single day in training then I will win that race.'

One pressure that Amy was blissfully unaware of was the weight of history. In ice sports, individual Olympic gold medals were won by UK figure skaters John Curry and Robin Cousins, who won gold in 1976 and 1980 respectively, and duo Jayne Torvill and Christopher Dean captivated the world with their *Bolero* on ice at the 1984 Sarajevo Olympics. Amy was just two years old at the time. Before her, no British woman had ever won gold in skeleton, and the only females that preceded her in an individual ice sport were the figure skater Madge Syers way back in 1908, and Jeannette Altwegg who became champion at the 1952 Winter Games in Oslo. The pair never met, and despite her success, Altwegg, who died in 2021 aged ninety, gave up skating soon after, in part due to injury but also because she opted for marriage and children. In an interview in 2011 she said, 'My family has been, and is, my career.'

Imagining someone like Altwegg stepping back into competition ice sports today, I reckon it would be unrecognizable. As Amy explains, athletes now have the benefit of teams of specialists and skates, sleds and sleighs that are precision-engineered. Her era was the turning point just before winter sports went high-tech. In fact, the sled that took her down the Whistler sliding track in Vancouver was a prototype built by post-graduate engineering students from Southampton University, designed as part of their doctoral thesis. Its development was funded by UK Sport alongside practical help from companies like BAE Systems and the McLaren Formula One team. And while Amy retired from the sport two years later, officially due to injury, she now reveals that it was also down to the politics of funding – having won gold and secured the sport's future, she believes she was then edged out of competition.

If I think of Lizzy Yarnold, the amount of runs down a track she did in her first year, probably took me four. Now, there's the best equipment, sled technicians and support that wasn't there in my era. You might have six cameras on the ice and several coaches, whereas I had one coach and one camera. The only moments that were ever filmed were your track entrance and exit on the training run. The speed at which people can learn these days is incredible. It's unbelievable how you can get better. After my win, new sleds came out but I wasn't allowed one. A new performance director came in and without a faster sled, I could not win races any more. I remember doing a race in La Plagne in France, and my push was the best in the world. I was physically the best in the world. My lines down the track were spot on, but I couldn't even get to the top twenty to get a second run in a race. Only the top twenty get the second run, and I remember the Germans coming up to me and saying, 'Amy. What's wrong with your equipment? What's wrong with your sled? You were the best athlete in the world, and you're not even getting in the top twenty.'

It was very bitter-sweet because by then I knew how to win races. I'd cracked my code. I knew I could win another medal in another Olympics but I was halfway through an Olympic cycle and I didn't have the best equipment. I had injuries that I suffered with every day and I realized I couldn't take that pain any longer unless I was winning. I'd spent my entire career never blaming my equipment for failure, but 100 per cent my equipment was not good. I never went public about it and if I had any regret in the whole of my career, it's that I didn't tell the truth. By then I was exhausted from it. In my opinion, the money went to the team below me. They needed a medal from that group of girls and they didn't need a medal from me. It made retiring so hard.

But I do believe that success breeds success. I read that Lizzy Yarnold said that because I won that gold, it proved it wasn't impossible. She could do it, too. And if I hadn't won, people wouldn't think they could, and that's really important. When new people come into the women's sport, we now have a history of winning medals and that's a very strong thing.

When I ask Amy about the injuries she has sustained over the years, the list would make most people wince. She has degenerative bulging discs in her back and neck and in the past has endured daily epidurals. She still has nerve root blocks to relieve the pain – a whole career of discomfort that she dates back to a crash in 2002. Her knees have also taken a hammering. She's already had four operations which means she can't jog for more than 3km or cycle for too long, and even then it takes her around four days to recover. She lives in a bungalow so she doesn't have to climb stairs, but still works out in her home gym, lifting up to 40kg on a bar and doing squats.

Yet none of that has put Amy off high-adrenaline sports. A second career beckoned not long after her retirement from skeleton when former driver and motor racing pundit Tony Jardine asked her to be his rally co-driver – a sport she now loves, but one she hilariously describes as 'fairly slow'. The task of taking pace notes, learning and understanding the detail of each track, controlling the time and the route of the driver isn't a million miles away from her obsessive preparation honed in skeleton. More recently she took part in a motorbike track day at Donington Park, an experience she is still not sure about due to her self-confessed lack of planning.

I have never been more petrified because while I've ridden bikes before, I didn't know those bikes. It was the lack of preparation that made me even more scared, but there was that pride that you feel afterwards: I did it and I'm so proud of myself. The chat that went on in my brain that day was probably bigger than at any time during my entire athletic career. I was out of my comfort zone. When I took the corners all I kept thinking was, 'Oh, my word! I'm cacking myself, but I'm doing it. I'm doing it.'

Was that same internal voice ever-present during her skeleton races? Yes, Amy tells me, but it quietened as she progressed and became more confident. Then, it was all about perfecting her speed, her movement and her mental outlook. All that meticulous groundwork to clinch gold by a winning margin of 0.56 seconds against German rival Kerstin Szymkowiak. What did it mean to her to hold that GB flag that day? And when she looks back now is the pain worth it?

Having the GB flag on me was really important. I don't know where that comes from, but I was always so proud that I got to have Great Britain written on the back of my coat. I knew I was the best in the country. That's just a really special thing, a magical thing. And to be able to see your flag up on a podium and sing your national anthem, it was something inside of me.

I wish I could relive it and feel it all over again. If a genie with a lamp came along and gave me a wish, it would be to go back, slow it down and take it all in, all the madness. You think you're going to remember every second, but you don't. Has it all been worth it? Yes, gold is always worth it.

CHAPTER 3

Unlocking Potential

Dame Katherine Grainger

ROWER, AND CURRENT CHAIR OF UK SPORT

'We've seen huge steps forward and we need to acknowledge and celebrate those incredible changes, but it's not done. It's a good start.'

Every week at Bisham Abbey, the state-of-the-art sports centre in Berkshire where the GB hockey team trained, we sat with our coach and ran through every match scenario. We'd have to imagine we were two goals down towards the end of an Olympic final – how were we going to level up the scores? Or we'd picture ourselves gripped by uncontrollable nerves before a match. How would we regain focus? All that testing and tweaking of our technique, thinking around our game strategy and honing our emotional responses got ironed out during each session. Those were tough, intensive days, but we worked through them as a team. It was at Bisham Abbey that I first saw Katherine Grainger. The National Sports Centre was also the training ground for British Rowing. In the aftermath of the Beijing Olympics in 2008, when the women's quadruple sculls (four rowers in each racing boat, each sculling two oars) of which she'd been a part narrowly missed out on a gold medal, I'd watch her in the gym. The clock was ticking down to London 2012 and Katherine was on a mission. Staring directly ahead, sweat pouring from her forehead, she glided back and forth on the rowing machine. The training looked lonely and uncompromising and I used to wonder what was going through her mind as she performed the same stroke over and over.

The session on the rowing machine was usually the middle session of a three-session training day. It could last between seventy-five and ninety minutes and we'd be tired from the early morning training, but knowing the end of the day was still a long way off. On the machine there is no one to talk to and very little to look at. Only a small screen telling you how fast – or not – you're going. It's relentless. Physically it can feel hard from the first second to the last, so people got through it in different ways. There was always music playing, or people were locked into their headphones. Of course there was time to think about technique and tactics, to relive past races or visualize races to come. But even that couldn't fill the hours, so we all had our own ways to distract our minds from the physical stress. One girl I rowed

with was a linguist and she would count up and down to 100 in
as many different languages as she could. Anna, whom I would
later partner in London 2012, was a mathematician and solved
mathematical problems in her head. And I was a fan of TV box
sets. I would watch dramas then try to recount word for word
what had happened. Admittedly it was a bit of a useless talent,
but I had an ear for it.

Listening to Katherine now, I understand more the intense highs
and lows of a rowing career; that concentration of training
through dark, cold winters in the gym, or out on the water, with
all your hopes pinned on a handful of events come the summer
season. In team sports, a loss at a World Championships or
an Olympics is emotionally shattering, but as a team you have
many more opportunities to practise and compete together.
For rowers, everything you've ever worked for builds to a few
nail-biting minutes where futures are made or broken.

Rowing is a crazy sport in some ways. You compete maybe four
times a year and for the rest of the time there's vast amounts
of training. Usually, I'd train from 7.15 a.m. to 4 p.m. from
September through to August, with only a few weeks broken
up by domestic trials or an international competition. We were
quite jealous of sports where people competed week in, week
out. Being in a sport with months of not competing can put
huge amounts of pressure on those moments of competition
because they are so rare and so short.

It's why you experience such dramatic emotions afterwards because everything leads to one event. On that one day you're not always going to feel great, have eaten well or have slept deeply. You might be carrying an injury; there might be a new line-up in the crew that's not quite tested enough. Irrespective of that, what you get good at is delivering on the day. It's a sport where you are utterly dependent on the people in your boat and they are utterly dependent on you. If anyone is having a bad day, that's the level the boat is at. It's a heavy responsibility and a responsibility I loved. Whether as a novice or as a senior athlete I never wanted to let anyone down. Everyone knew what your crew-mates had been through to get to that point and so you wanted to be sure to help them get the best possible result.

That fear of letting others down is a sentiment you will hear from every athlete. It can cripple us regardless of whether you compete as an individual, in pairs, fours or eights as Katherine did, or in a larger team. Panic still runs through me whenever I relive the moment I conceded a penalty to the Dutch not long after I came on to the pitch in our Olympic final in Rio – the only time I'd given away a penalty in my entire international career. If we'd lost, it wouldn't just have been myself I'd have let down, it would have been everyone in the team, the whole country even. Also on your mind are the people who have supported you throughout your whole career – parents perhaps, or teachers or coaches. For Katherine it was a succession of people who helped unlock her potential. But it all began with a girl from her university rowing club.

I'd just started a law degree at Edinburgh University and it was freshers' week. There were all sorts of stands and you could join exciting-sounding new clubs like Ultimate Frisbee and juggling. I joined the juggling club but I was with a friend from our halls of residence who wanted to talk to the rowing club. I sat clutching my juggling membership card when one of the senior rowers came up to me. She asked if I was interested in rowing. I said no, and explained that I was waiting for my friend. A few moments later she came back and asked again, 'Are you sure you don't want to join? I think you'd enjoy it and you'd be really good.' Again I said no. When she approached me a third time she suggested I should come along, learn a bit about it, meet some people and there was no commitment. And there'd be a free drink involved for new students. 'That's my kind of sport,' I thought. Looking back now I don't think it was rowing I fell in love with initially, it was the people and the environment. I met the most incredible group of women. They were strong characters: fun, passionate, committed and incredibly supportive. I'm now godmother to the kids of three of those women. I made friends for life.

In fact, Katherine's ambition for rowing turned out to be a slow burn. As far as she was concerned it was a sport she'd enjoy alongside her degree, but not something that would ever be her life's passion and certainly not earn her a living. It wasn't until her second year at university when she trialled for the senior women's rowing team that she hit a pivotal moment.

I was a successful novice in my first year, but when I trialled to be one of sixteen senior women, I got my first learning experience. The names were read out in front of everyone in one of the lecture halls. I was convinced I'd be picked and I was just waiting to hear which boat I was going to be selected for. But I wasn't in the first four, or the second four, or the third, or even the fourth. Basically, I was put into a new fifth boat they put together – there to make up the club's social numbers. I remember walking out of that hall feeling so upset and disappointed and really embarrassed. I'd got it so wrong.

I climbed up Arthur's Seat, the hill in Edinburgh where nobody should climb alone at night, but I was overwhelmed, just raging against myself and the world. I eventually said to myself, either I walk down this hill and never row again, or I accept my place near the bottom of the team and put the hard work in to see where I can get to. Afterwards I joined the fifth boat and slowly climbed the ladder, with a healthy dose of humility. I knew I had good physical attributes but my technical skill needed a lot of refining. I think the senior women saw that in me and a few of them took me on as their project. They were never nasty or competitive. It was all about bringing out my potential – balancing incredibly hard work with enjoyment and patience and understanding.

It's fascinating to hear Katherine talk about being exposed to the right mix of hard graft and support in the pursuit of excellence. In the elite environment, which is highly competitive, with high tension, high emotion and fast physical burn-out, it can be tough for mentors and coaches to get that balance right. At a time when accusations of bullying are increasing around the training of both male and female athletes, it's something I've reflected on in my own career. Without doubt, it's an environment where honest truths get delivered. And there were times when moments of my poor play were made an example of in front of the team in training. I considered it harsh, often unfair, but not bullying. That said, I do think women learn and respond differently to different styles of coaching. Perhaps women need more buy-in to a way of working. Having mostly been coached by men, I wanted to understand more of Katherine's experience.

My first real coach was a volunteer coach at Edinburgh called Hamish Burrell who went on to coach in the GB team. His understanding and insight in coaching women was amazing. He was a man of few words – very quiet and understated and a good listener. He had what would be described now as soft skills. He was someone who made me understand what would make me work as an athlete and as a person. He told me there would be three things in my life that would always compete. They might be different things at different times but at that moment it was my university work, my rowing and my personal life. Those things would rarely, if ever, be perfectly balanced so I shouldn't try to make them. I just needed to be aware of the balance, or imbalance, and how I was feeling about that. So if I was struggling with my training he took an interest in what was going on in the rest of my life. If I got frustrated on the water, he understood something else might be frustrating me with my course work or with friends or family. I hadn't appreciated how unusual his natural care was. And he took from other worlds all the time, areas outside of sport. He was always reading and learning and he fed my curious mind. I loved it. It was holistic and engaging and challenging. It was something I hadn't realized I needed and it made me better.

It was Hamish Burrell who also persuaded Katherine to trial for the British team, which was to mark the start of her international career. Again, she recalls him planting that seed in her head in a quiet and unassuming way.

In my fourth year, Hamish came up to me in the gym at the end of a rowing session. He said, 'I was thinking, the British trials are coming up in the new year. I wonder if you should think about going.' He said it with a very light touch and I remember almost falling off the machine. 'What? You have got to be joking!' He said, 'Just think about it. Let's chat next week. What's the worst that's going to happen? You've nothing to lose and you might gain something.' I knew if I went I'd be there alongside Olympians who had just come back from the Atlanta Games. But he said, 'They're not looking for the finished article. They're looking for people with potential which could be physical or emotional or tactical or strategic. They want someone they can craft.' It was really non-threatening. So I went to Henley and did my first trials. And my life changed.

Like any sporting career, there's hard work that goes into shaping raw talent, but for Katherine there was also some luck. When she went to those trials and got picked, the year was 1997. She went on to win the Under-23s World Rowing Championships in a coxless pair (two rowers, each holding one oar without a coxswain riding with them) with partner Francesca Zino, setting a new record for the event. But that was also the year that National Lottery funding for elite sport launched and began to transform UK sport.

In Atlanta the previous year, Team GB had finished thirty-sixth in the Olympic medal table with just fifteen medals and only one gold – won in rowing by Sir Steve Redgrave and Sir Matthew Pinsent. Something needed to change fast and the funding that the Lottery provided did just that. Fast-forward twenty years to Rio when I won gold, and Great Britain was positioned second in the medal table after its most successful games.

For women's sport in particular, Lottery funding became a game-changer. It had never been adequately resourced and many sports relied on pockets of funding, the enthusiasm of lone benefactors or athletes supporting themselves. Crucially, after the funding body UK Sport was formed around the same time, funding decisions became gender-blind – allocating money to disciplines rather than to men's or women's sports. Now, as a former competitor and current chair of UK Sport, I was interested to hear how Katherine felt the impact of sustained investment helped women like her.

When I was back at Edinburgh University, there were some amazing women like Dot Blackie who had gone on to row at Olympic level, but at university level there was a hierarchy. Rowing boats are expensive and back then the men would get the best boats, the new boats. When they were finished with them the women's team would get them. We were very strong, opinionated women, but it's almost as if we'd accepted that was the way it was. We were equal in numbers and could easily have had a voice, but for some reason we didn't use it.

When I came into international competition, the top medals were being won by the men's team. Steve Redgrave and Matthew Pinsent were dominant in the sport and the success brought sponsorship and coverage. That didn't feel unfair. It is probably unsurprising that there would be increased media attention and sponsorship for World and Olympic champions, especially when we had far fewer across all sports then than we have now. The hard challenge was for anyone trying to get a foothold to begin that climb. The women's rowing team had always had impressive, talented, competitive athletes, but needed help to make the step up to international level. I massively credit the National Lottery with enabling that step up. By pure chance, my arrival in the sport was timed perfectly. Because Steve and Matt were repeated gold medallists, had delivered time and time again, and were aiming for the next Olympics in Sydney, rowing was a sport that proved it could consistently perform at the top level and was a solid investment. The lead-up to Sydney 2000 was the first time the women rowers had full-time paid coaches, a funded programme and a main training base, and those things undoubtedly added to the ingredients for success.

Katherine also recalls that it was in the run-up to those Sydney Games when she encountered a second coach who was also to be an influence on her: Ron Needs. He was quiet and uncompromising, she says, but had a knack of balancing hard work with enjoyment, and also had a 'magic touch' when it came to working with women. Ron had previously coached the women's rowing squad at Cambridge, leading them to win the Boat Race ten times in eleven years and, at the same time, establishing a development pathway to international competition. Under his leadership, Katherine became one of the women's eight who clinched bronze at the World Championships in France in 1997.

At that year's World Championships, Ron coached the four and the eight. He'd been a businessman and before the Lottery came in he was contributing his own funding to rowing. He had been very supportive to development groups and to Commonwealth teams, and when the Olympic team were unfunded he had contributed to that as well. He was one of those amazing people who didn't just contribute their time to sport. I always got on well with Ron. He was in his seventies and we loved his retro GB tracksuits that served as a good reminder of his long history of being a coach. He had vast experience of coaching different teams and once again he had this very strong, very vocal group of women around him. He was quite short, too, and we were all physically imposing. But he handled us beautifully. He let us indulge in a lot of fun and 1997 was the year the Spice Girls exploded. We transformed his truck into a 'girl power' truck. He didn't have much say in it. I like to think he enjoyed it.

He was a hard coach and a tough coach, unafraid to deliver the difficult message, but a coach with a twinkle in his eye. He encouraged fun and a little bit of mayhem up to a point. He understood the outlet we needed in the depths of intense training or after big senior championships and allowed that side of us to flourish. And I think he genuinely enjoyed female company. He had experiences and understood life beyond sport and he was worldly wise in that way.

Over the next decade, Katherine would go on to win silver in the quadruple sculls at the Sydney Games in 2000 and silver again in the coxless pairs in Athens four years later. But fast-forward to 2008, the year before I saw Katherine training at Bisham Abbey, and the unthinkable had happened for the women's team at the Beijing Olympics. In the quadruple sculls the crew had led for three quarters of the race, but in the last

500 metres their Chinese rivals put on a sprint that Team GB had never witnessed before. In the final finish the Chinese boat came in an agonizing half-length ahead.

When I watch that race now, I remember at the time how my heart dropped to my feet. The exhaustion and utter devastation on the faces of the women's team was so tough to see. It's an emotion we've all had to learn to deal with, but to have trained for four years, to have come that tantalizingly close only to see your dream evaporate in seconds, must have been gutting. Katherine didn't know it then, but she would have another attempt at gold four years later. How did Katherine feel and how did she bounce back to begin on another Olympic cycle?

It wasn't until we crossed the line when we knew in that instant it was over. The years leading up to that moment had always been about continual improvement until the Beijing final, how we could keep getting better for those Olympics and deliver our best performance in that final race. We had won multiple World Championships and had our mind focused on the ultimate result in Beijing. Then suddenly you've crossed the line and there are no more chances to get better. It was the end of the campaign. It was done.

In that moment I felt I'd let down everyone who, up to that point, had contributed to delivering in Beijing. We'd failed them. But when you compete at that level, your perspective has shifted. In fact, you don't really have perspective. The competition is everything. It's all you think about. It's all anyone talks to you about. This is what you are and what you do and now you haven't delivered it. I remember when I came home I didn't even want to walk down the high street. I didn't want to look people in the eye. It was my own skewed perspective, because people were unbelievably lovely and constantly trying to say 'It's okay' and that it was still an excellent result. It just didn't feel that way to me. It took brilliant people – family and friends who were patient, loving and supportive. And ultimately time is indeed the greatest healer. I went away on holiday for a chunk of time and that's where I found perspective again. No one talked about the Olympics. No one was really aware of the Olympics and I realized, it's what I do, it's not who I am. There are wonderful places where it didn't matter and no one cared if I'd won gold or if I'd never sat in a boat. Sometimes you need reminding that the world is bigger. But for that period of time you are absorbed by it, and it feels like everything.

That second chance Katherine was given turned out to be the happiest three years of her rowing career, she tells me. A partnership with fellow Olympian Anna Watkins, who had taken bronze in the double sculls in Beijing with Elise Laverick, became one of the most iconic pairings the women's sport has ever seen. When she and Watkins first joined together to compete in the 2010 World Championships in New Zealand, they remained unbeaten for the whole season, and the season after that. In my experience, that chemistry is almost inexplicable. As a hockey team we had felt it in the run-up to Rio in 2016, but no amount of analysis could truly explain it. Likewise, Katherine and Anna just clicked. They realized the potential in each other from the outset and nurtured it. But what was it that made them so special?

Anna and I had been on the team together for a while and she'd suggested the year before that we should try a boat together, but I was still coming to terms with Beijing. Then, when we were at a training camp in Portugal, we were put together in a double. It's one of those moments that's imprinted on my mind. We took about ten strokes and we stopped. I turned and said, 'Wow.' And Anna looked at me and said, 'I know.' Our coach arrived in the motorboat, impatient for us to get on with it and asked what we were chatting about. We said, 'It just feels so good.' We'd both had this moment of something being incredible. It was so cohesive and powerful. We were both very strong. So often you can move towards physical, powerful rowing but it can look a bit ungainly and inefficient. Or you get people who row beautifully but not powerfully. We seemed to have the makings of both: we had the power and the technique. We moved so similarly and with the same rhythm. It was so simple and so easy. It was like magic. So it got really exciting from early on. We began to ask, 'What's the potential in this? Where could we take this?' It felt like we could try different things, play and explore and test it. At some point every day we told each other how lucky we were. We really appreciated every day together, the fun we had, the speed we had, the potential and opportunity it gave us. We felt like we could play on the water every day, and we won every race we ever competed in.

So, did she and Anna also have to share the same perspective to become such a perfect pairing?

Anna and I were actually quite different in the way we approached things. She's an incredible mathematician with a very analytical brain. When we did sessions we'd often have lots of instruments on the boat to measure things like depth, range, length, angle and power output. We had printouts that were packed with numbers and graphs. Anna would sit and soak it all up and in an instant could understand why something was happening, where the potential was and how we could improve it. Whereas I looked at it and thought, 'Well those are some very pretty patterns.' I was more instinctive in the feel of the boat. I couldn't always explain why we were going fast or why we should try something different, but somehow I could sense it. Anna would know instantly the words and the facts behind it and always came to the same answers just through a different means. It gave us a huge appreciation for each other's skills and abilities and also even more confidence that between us we would have things covered.

We were different in some of our ways of thinking, but we were also so similar in attitude and humour and style that it made it ridiculously fun. Anna let me play. She understood the pressure and how serious Beijing had felt, but also that I'm at my best when I can have fun. She was good at unlocking that. She brought out the best in me.

When something feels that right, the tension building to the 2012 London Olympics must have been both exciting and excruciating. Entering into an Olympics knowing it may be your only opportunity to right the wrongs of the past feels a pressure like no other. It's no wonder that in training Katherine looked so focused. Thankfully, it's a goal she got to realize. For the first time since 1976, the year women's rowing entered the Olympic programme, British women won Olympic gold. And not just one. Katherine and Anna became women's rowing's second ever British gold medallists – the first being won only two days earlier on Dorney Lake when Helen Glover and Heather Stanning took gold in the women's coxless pairs. One day later Kat Copeland and Sophie Hosking also triumphed at the lightweight double sculls. In that bumper year, it seemed like women's potential that had been building for decades was finally being unleashed.

The night before our race at the 2012 Olympics I said to our coach Paul Thompson, 'I believe we can do this,' and he asked me why I thought that. I didn't have an answer other than a very strong feeling. The feeling was strong, but it was vague, whereas Anna had analysed the detail. She took massive confidence from me because of how I was feeling and my instincts, and I took massive confidence from her because I utterly trusted her ability to understand, process and be entirely honest with what that told her. Between us we didn't want any chinks in the armour, and on the eve of the Olympics it felt like we had everything covered. That was exciting.

I remember thinking that I would have rather died that day than let her down. Now, it sounds overly dramatic but that's how I felt. I would have put myself through anything physically not to let her down. Paul was integral to our success too. He was as excited as us about the new levels we could take our sport to. He loved our ambition and encouraged our enjoyment of it, and he wanted to lift the standard of his coaching too. Between us we felt we could deliver something special. And then there was the boat. Anna and I felt strongly that the boat deserved to be the fastest thing on the planet, and it was our responsibility to make it fly. We asked, 'What can we do to make sure it fulfils its potential?' It felt like a massive privilege. That boat was ours to win the Olympics.

But if London 2012 was a bumper year for rowing, it was also a bumper year for women's sport overall. It was the first ever Olympics where every sport had women's representation and women took 39 per cent of the medal haul. Women like heptathlete Jessica Ennis, boxer Nicola Adams, cyclist Laura Trott and equestrian Charlotte Dujardin, as well as female rowers like Katherine were all catapulted to gold-medal status and household names. Of course, amazing women had gone before, but at last it felt like women's sport was gaining traction with the media. Many of us hoped sponsorship deals might follow, which have been historically pitiful for women, and I recall this tremendous atmosphere of everyone wanting to keep the momentum going. In its wake, Katherine became one of many women's voices calling for better sports programmes aimed at schoolgirls, more female leadership in sports organizations and more opportunities for women to get involved in sport. Given her hopes then for the future, I wondered what she thinks of the Games' legacy now?

That year did feel like a shift. Previously, you sometimes heard the attitude being expressed that people didn't want to read about, or follow, women's sport. But 2012 was amazing. The front pages as well as the back pages of newspapers were frequently dominated by women's sport. It was instinctive and natural, and there were many breakthroughs. The frustration is that it felt it would be a complete game-changer, but I don't necessarily think it has been in every sense. Things have undoubtedly improved and continue to improve, but women's sport is still drastically underrepresented in many ways. We've seen huge steps forward and we need to acknowledge and celebrate those incredible changes, but it's not done. It's a good start.

Now, through her leadership role as Chair of UK Sport since 2017, Katherine has found herself in a more strategic position to champion the rise of women in all aspects, whether it's on the track, the lake, as a coach, or in other leadership or decision-making roles. In particular, having been inspired by the coaches who unlocked her potential, she has been keen to promote more women into coaching careers. However, just as National Lottery funding provided a mechanism to support women's sport twenty-five years ago, she believes that cultural barriers are only broken when time, resource and focus is put into understanding how they can be broken.

I would love to see more female coaches in our sports. You do see good numbers of women at junior levels but they don't always filter through to the top. I only had one female coach across my twenty-year international career. There are a whole host of reasons why there are so few, and making sure we really understand the complexities of that will help us to address the numbers. Some of it is environment and culture, and some practical challenges. In previous studies we have seen that the vast amount of time away from home can become prohibitive, especially for women who have childcare or care roles. It's also often still seen as a very male environment and some women will ask if they want to be one of the only females in that set-up. If there are barriers, or even perceived barriers for women coming into coaching, then we have to ask how we can start changing that to create a more balanced environment. Women have proved they can be incredible coaches. It's about listening and finding out what the blocking points are, or what might be putting people off the role. UK Sport have run a number of programmes for developing female coaches and we have exceptional top-level female coaches who help to mentor, advise and support in those programmes. Having that supportive network can help to make a real positive difference. It's the same as finding athletes – there is so much potential out there, we all need to do what we can to encourage, nurture and develop the talent to become brilliant in their own right. And we need to make sure we tell the stories of existing female coaches, who are excellent role models.

In hockey, I've seen myself how better funding and a continued focus can change a team into a winning team with a winning culture, but does Katherine think it's always about the money?

Changing narratives doesn't always start with funding, but what we've seen through the National Lottery is the vast opportunity it gives people. It opens doors. But things can be changed in other ways, for example at the policy level. Title IX in the USA is a great example. It's a law that was brought in over fifty years ago to make sure there was no sex discrimination in any school or any education programme that receives funding from the federal government. It meant that schools, colleges and universities had to provide equal funding for men's and women's sports. It was recently reported that before Title IX was passed, only 1 per cent of college athletic budgets went to women's sports programmes. So policies and laws can help redress imbalance.

The media also plays an important role and bears a huge responsibility for the stories it tells, and also who tells those stories. And for all the challenges of social media, it has created a platform where voices can be heard, where female athletes have found a space where they can talk about themselves and their sport, but also issues that are important to them. In recent years we have seen more high-profile female athletes talking about pregnancy, motherhood, menstruation and body image as well as passions on societal issues ranging from climate change to sustainability to racism and poverty. They have influence and want to use that to help make positive change.

I also think we have made progress with recognizing the importance of having women in decision-making roles, of having a place and a voice. There is plenty of work still to be done, plenty of challenges that we know about, and more that we don't know about yet, but I know there are brilliant people with the passion and the drive to make it all happen. It's a fantastic time for women's sport, and there is so much aspiration, inspiration and possibility.

Katherine, who has broken so many barriers, remains one of the most down-to-earth and humble people I know. Her success happened through sheer grit and determination, but she is also the first to acknowledge that her remarkable story would not have happened without the support she got early on and throughout her career. Her sporting life also seems dusted by a sprinkling of serendipity – opportunities that presented themselves at the right time, which she grabbed with both hands. Every moment since has been a learning curve, she tells me.

I am forever grateful to that senior student at freshers' week who saw something in me and was persistent enough to come back three times to get me involved in rowing. For all its ego and ambition and drive to achieve, sport keeps you very modest. It asks the most of you in every sense: physically, mentally and emotionally. It teaches you the skills to work with others, to bring out the best in people, and to find fun in the smallest moments. It helps you to problem-solve with every new challenge you face and to cope with pressure and with the inevitable disappointments, finding ways to make yourself better as a result – you name it, you learn it. The life lessons are constant and the friends are forever. Sport has asked the most of me and brought out the best in me. Sometimes, I do have a sliding doors moment when I think, 'What would my life have been like if I'd done something else? What if I hadn't gone to the freshers' fair?' I think I will be forever grateful that sport found me.

CHAPTER 4

Never Give Up

Dame Sarah Storey

PARALYMPIAN CYCLIST

*'Having my children with me makes me a
stronger athlete and a more reliable athlete.'*

Sarah Storey may have notched up seventeen golds, eight silvers
and three bronze medals at successive Paralympic Games, plus
more than forty medals at World Championships, but she's not
giving up. In the month that we speak, she's just returned from
successfully defending her title in the individual pursuit event
against France's Heidi Gaugain at the World Championships
in Paris. Gaugain, only seventeen years old at the time of
competing, is a fresh face on the Paralympic cycling track.
Aged forty-five, Sarah is the grande dame of the sport.

Speaking personally, as a former Team GB member now

playing hockey at club level, I know that seven years after my own Olympic victory, I still have that killer instinct – that competitive edge against younger players that makes me think, 'You're not getting past me.' But being the UK's most decorated Paralympian, I'd be forgiven for thinking that Sarah might be satisfied with getting to a final, perhaps clinching a silver. I could not be more wrong. In a career that has spanned thirty years and counting, Sarah remains a one-woman medal factory, slugging every race out to the death.

It's harder than people realize to stay at the top because everyone is trying to beat you. Heidi is part of the French national team and trying to follow my example, and I was really hoping that at some point before my career ends I would get to race her one-on-one, and I did. I am clearly the oldest in the field and she's certainly the youngest, and it gives me goosebumps to think that someone is attempting to emulate me. But I went out to catch her. I got in there, in the same straight within the first kilometre and then I had to hold her there. I was completely on the edge of blowing up, but I thought, there's absolutely no way we're going the full three kilometres. I'm going to catch you. It's the way I've always ridden my finals: I go out to catch my competitor and it's what inspired me to ride the individual pursuit because it's one-on-one. She was a bit mortified, to be honest.

In women's cycling, the individual pursuit is raced over three kilometres. Each rider begins at the same time and tries to catch the other who starts at the opposite side of the track. For spectators like me, it's one of the most exhilarating events to watch in the velodrome. The pace is blistering; the roar of the crowd deafening. And Sarah, who began her cycling career on the track, knows only too well that to get to her level of world-beating you have to compete against the best, learn from the best and lose to the best.

At Heidi's age, it's all about experience. She has a huge future, but the best lessons you learn are by racing the best in your category. Ultimately, it's how I started in cycling. I came in from swimming, where I was the matriarch. In cycling I was a complete nobody and very quickly I realized I needed to race the best in the world and get beaten big-time to improve and get on to that winning streak. It's a pleasure to be able to dish out that same menu I wanted to devour myself when I was younger.

That Sarah has never lost that hunger shows a resilience honed over decades. And if there's one word that resonated with me when I understood more of her story, it's endurance. Now classified in the Paracycling C5 category, having been born without a functioning left hand, Sarah competed against able-bodied kids throughout her early years. She describes her school, Disley Primary School on the edge of the Peak District, as very 'sports-oriented'. The headmaster even set up the school's own swimming club where Sarah excelled before going on to train at

Stockport Metro Swimming Club. What began as her wanting to dip her toe into Paralympic swimming as an eleven-year-old set her on a trajectory to her first Paralympics at breakneck speed.

I saw something on the North West News about a girl who was trying to qualify for the Paralympic Games. She had an arm amputation of some kind and I remember asking my swimming coach, who himself had been a deaf Olympian swimmer, how it worked if you had a part of your limb missing. I'd never really contemplated it, because I'd always competed in able-bodied sport. I was county table tennis champion. I played on the county netball team. I was also a cross-country runner for English Schools so it had never been factored in. I just competed against other kids.

He said, 'Well, there's a classification system and you would fall into that.' He put me in touch with a lady whom I literally wrote to every time I did a personal best time in the pool. Eventually, around eighteen months later, she sent me some information about a swimming gala that was a qualifier for the National Championships. I went in the summer of 1991, but when I got there it was more like a rehabilitation session for people with injuries and disability. Back then, there was a much closer link between this activity-based rehab and the competition pathway – an attempt to develop a pathway before there was funding. But I felt very out of place. I drifted up and down the pool.

However, there was an amazing lady there called Trina Curran who ran Manchester Kestrels Sports Club for the Disabled. I told her, 'I don't think Paralympics is for me. It's not what I was expecting. I don't need rehab. I need to race.' She explained that a competition format did exist but that I needed to go to the National Swimming Centre in Birmingham. When I joined that competition training squad I started in the slowest lane and ended up in the fastest. That weekend, I was invited on to the British team to start training.

It took me until I was aged nineteen to earn my first international cap and another eight years until I was aged twenty-seven to win gold. In truth, I found competing at that level daunting at first – no one takes any prisoners and when you are out on the pitch you are expected to do your job. But I had worked my way up through the junior ranks, so while I felt better prepared I was also gripped by fear of failure. But Sarah's journey to her first gold at the Paralympic Games in Barcelona in 1992 can only be described as stratospheric. Ten months is all it took between that invitation in Birmingham and her dominating in backstroke and individual medley. She was one of the youngest in the team, aged just fourteen.

What also amazes me is that in 1991, Paralympic sport was not embedded in mainstream consciousness whatsoever. She had no Para heroes or heroines to emulate. Instead, she set her sights on Sarah Hardcastle, the Olympian swimmer ten years her senior, who specialized in 400 and 800 metre freestyle and

also competed in medley races. For Sarah, it was Hardcastle's
focus and individuality that stood out. She was disciplined.
She kept her head down in the water, doggedly following the
black line for the duration of every race. Although the pair did
not meet until years later, Sarah says watching her inspired
her to become self-motivated and also led her to latch on to
other mentors at the club of a similar age to Hardcastle who
could give her one-to-one support. Competing most of her
life against able-bodied swimmers also gave her an edge and
a better grounding in the discipline, she explains.

*I had so much experience of competing and being not quite
good enough, so I had this idea that I always needed to do that
little bit extra. That provided me with a really good work ethic
when it came to suddenly being thrust into an international
environment. And other swimmers advised me, 'Just treat it
like another competition.' So, I think I'd always had that very
strong sense of self and a focused mindset. Even though TV
cameras from* Blue Peter *were following me around, I was able
to focus. When I won I was so excited. I nearly fell off the
podium in front of the Queen of Spain. It just felt amazing,
almost like this sense of disbelief. I thought, this is so good;
I want it to last forever. I never realized I'd still be here eight
Paralympic Games later.*

But that level of resilience is rarely built through sport alone
and while Sarah was smashing it in the pool, winning golds,

three silvers and a bronze in Barcelona, her school mates interpreted her success differently. She got bullied not because of her physical difference but because she'd set her teenage self on a different pathway. From experience, not being part of the pack is one of the hardest things teenagers pursuing sport have to deal with. Certainly when I was at school there were classmates who never understood what I was doing and to what level I was doing it at, and if I wasn't going out to parties or into town with them I was labelled a 'hockey geek'.

To cope with the bullying, Sarah says she learned how to become laser-focused. Now, she says, she would reassure her fourteen-year-old self that the experience would build her character and give her empathy, but at the time it took its toll.

At netball, initially kids thought it was best not to throw to me because I might not catch the ball, but they soon realized I was the safest pair of hands on the court. I was very dexterous and I could throw and catch a ball as well as anyone, and also catch with two hands. At school level my disability made no difference in the sporting environment. But in the normal teenage girl environment, I was always away at weekends. I was always at a training camp. I was always at a competition. Swimming is a really demanding sport and I'd arrive at school with wet hair and when I came home from the Games in 1992 I never did a full week at school. There was always something that took me out of school for at least one day, so I became a part-timer.

I was also thrust into this limelight. One minute I was choosing my GCSE options and then I was rubbing shoulders with other gold medallists like Sally Gunnell, Linford Christie, Colin Jackson and Paralympians like Tanni Grey-Thompson. Although I had a relationship with teachers and the senior leaders at the school about how my education would be managed around the demands of being an international athlete, not everyone gets that memo, so kids asked, why is she different? Eventually I twigged what was happening because I'd hear girls in the toilets talking about me: 'Who does she think she is? Look at the state of her with her wet hair!' The bullying was exclusionary. I'd walk into a room and it would fall silent or girls would move to make sure I was sitting by myself. I used to leave school at lunchtime and I stopped eating properly. It was a cry for help, but I never let it outwardly bother me. Having an eating disorder was me wanting an element of control. I didn't have control over the girls, but I did have control over my training and eating. Now, in sport we come across eating disorders all the time and I think it's provided me with strength and understanding, but also a clarity and a credibility to speak to someone who might be struggling. I understand why it might be happening.

At some point I realized that one bad day would be over and the next day would be different, or I'd be somewhere different. My friendship group and all those people whom I was training with away from school were very different with me. I was always treated as I would hope to have been treated.

For the next twelve years, Sarah was to compete as a Paralympian swimmer, clocking up medal after medal. But progressive ear infections, which would have made her deaf had she not stopped, prompted her to switch to the cycling track. Unbelievably, she mirrored her rapid success in the pool. In the run-up to the Commonwealth Games Trials she was being kept out of the water, so British Cycling trialled her over 3000 metres on the velodrome. The next day, she came second in a race, just outside the world record. Three weeks later, she raced over 3000 metres on the track at the Open European Championships and broke the world record, also winning gold in the 500 metres time trial. Days later at the same event she competed on the road and won gold in the road race and silver in the road time trial. To describe Sarah as a machine would be no understatement, but I was fascinated by how she could learn a completely new sport in such a short time frame.

I'd not raced before but I'd watched a lot, and I'm very analytical. I'd looked at the mechanics of races, so I'd done a lot of homework. I knew that every time a rider passed the pits, you'd get instructions shouted at you. I knew that if somebody tried to break away, I needed to cover that move. I got to the front and just went as hard as I could. I had nothing to lose. I'd spent my whole life racing and it was that raw capability that worked. There needed to be a lot of refinement to me physically: I had massive shoulders from swimming and a completely different body shape to how I am today. But in terms of that intrinsic motivation and determination and racecraft, I had it.

What was really hard was the endurance side of it. The road time trial had been around twenty-seven minutes and, bearing in mind I didn't like doing anything over 400 metres freestyle in the pool, and had only ever swum 800 metres because I had to, I went out far too hard. I died a death and sort of crept over the line. Learning to pace myself was a big thing, and that took a long time. Even today there are times when I go out too hard. But now, I've got that experience of not completely dying on my feet.

For cyclists, dying on their feet can finish a race there and then. What Sarah described as almost 'blowing up' in her tussle with Heidi Gaugain at the World Championships is also known in the sport as 'bonking' – the moment all professional cyclists dread: sudden extreme lethargy, blurred vision, muscles shot through and an inability to continue. It's caused by glycogen depletion – in other words, low blood sugar – and it can take you from flying high to falling hard in a matter of minutes. Sarah explains that what ultimately helped her win more on the track was training longer distances on the road, which she began after the Beijing Olympics in 2008.

But endurance cycling isn't just psychologically challenging, it's physically incredibly demanding. Yet training for longer periods at a lower intensity develops a rider's physiology. Their bodies adapt to use fat as their primary source of fuel before the body switches to its more limited source of glucose stored in the body's muscles. In cycling-speak, it's called having more left in the tank.

For Sarah, she also had to learn to ride both on the track and on the road while taking into consideration her added physical complications. Because of her deformed left hand, she naturally has less balance and control compared to her Olympian counterparts, and has had to adapt to riding on an adjusted bike that has its brakes and gears positioned only on the right-hand side.

I realized that if I wanted to be better at the individual pursuit on the track I needed to be better on the road, and so I started to explore that opportunity. I did my first professional road race in the UCI women's peloton in 2010, and I started to look at road racing teams and racing at high levels in the women's peloton.

I always said that when I came into cycling I wanted to be judged on the same physical scores that the Olympic programme use because I knew that on a static bike I needed to be physically and physiologically as good as them. This was so that when it came to overcoming the technical differences of handling a bike with one set of brakes and gears it became a technical challenge and not a physiological challenge.

Road racing is like a game of chess on a bike. It's made to look very easy on TV, but it's another level of competition. It's very exciting. You need mental capacity to concentrate on what's happening around you. You have to be able to read a

race. *You have to know all of the other riders in the peloton
and what their strengths and weaknesses are. And who's who
in that race because their numbers change. There are so many
things to think about, it can be an overwhelming experience.*

*And the length of the race means that you need more blood
capillaries. Over time you develop a bigger tank to work with,
and so that enables you to work longer in the aerobic zone
before you get to your anaerobic and your capacity zones,
needed for hard sprints. The fitter you are, the greater your
aerobic capacity. I always come back to the track in much
better shape if I've been out on the road because that's where
you gain physical fitness.*

*And once you've mastered the craft of the track, you learn
how to ride on the steep bank and transition between the
different gradients and work with the speed, you don't need a
huge amount of time to prepare.*

If that doesn't sound tough enough, imagine doing all of that
when you're pregnant – which is exactly what Sarah went on
to do. Having a longer career inevitably results in sportswomen
hitting more of life's milestones that in the past have prompted
some very hard choices for women when it comes to having
a family.

I had my two kids, Molly and Zac, after retiring from
international hockey. In team sport more than in individual
disciplines, becoming pregnant would have ended my career
there and then because of the perceived impact that may have on

a team. It's something that I hope will change in the future and certainly by the end of my career, members of the GB team were looking to the Australian women's team, the Hockeyroos, as an example because a couple of its players had taken maternity leave and returned to the sport. But I know it's still the case that pregnancy and motherhood can feel like a taboo for elite sportswomen and many women fear a loss in funding if they fall pregnant while still competing. Sarah became pregnant and gave birth while still training and racing, and I can only take my hat off to her. Pregnancy can feel like a marathon for all women, but add to that the potential risks that come with elite sports – maintaining nutrients and oxygen to the baby for starters. When it comes to birth, our pelvic floor muscles are often too well developed to deliver naturally, resulting in a higher likelihood of Caesarean section which can increase recovery times. Plus, there's the surge in hormones, which admittedly left me a blubbering wreck, and that can also increase the risk of injury, in particular the hormone relaxin which loosens muscles and ligaments in preparation for birth.

Yet trailblazing women have led the way. In 2014 long-distance runner Jo Pavey became the oldest woman at forty to win gold at a European Championships, ten months after giving birth to her second child. Jessica Ennis-Hill took silver in Rio in 2016 after the birth of her son, Reggie. And wheelchair racer Tanni Grey-Thompson won the London Marathon ten weeks after giving birth to her daughter. Hard to think that it was only as recently as 2021 that funding body UK Sport issued its first official guidance on managing pregnancy. Certainly, I know women athletes often shy away from discussing the impact it can have on their bodies and their careers, so I was interested whether Sarah's experience had been a positive one.

In 2012 I'd won four gold medals at the London Olympics and I'd become a dame. I considered everything after that to be a bonus. Louisa arrived nine months after the games. I didn't know if I was going to carry on, but during pregnancy I went out to Lanzarote to keep training as I was still being funded. And there was no real question that I wasn't good enough to be funded throughout my pregnancies. Obviously in my second pregnancy, I had the example of my first to say 'I'm coming back and I'm going to race and I'm going to win you medals.'

I researched how to stay fit and healthy and cycling is good exercise because there's no impact. And I was lucky with both pregnancies that I didn't suffer any morning sickness or any kind of adverse effects with the additional hormones. I had to limit some of the strength-based work where you hold your breath, but because I have a large aerobic tank I can do more without going into any sort of oxygen debt. And there were techniques like checking you could still talk while you are training to check you were not in oxygen debt.

Being heavier and having to push that weight up hills was more annoying. To cope with my growing bump I adapted my bike position and used what's called an Ergostem, which allowed me to fit the space to the bump. With Louisa I trained right up until the day of my contractions.

With my second baby Charlie, whom I gave birth to after the Rio Paralympics in 2016, I raced until I was around twenty weeks pregnant. I was massive second time around so it became harder to race upright.

In fact, Sarah describes birth and the adjustment to motherhood as having more impact on her. I also wondered if, like so many women, she suffered the mum guilt of juggling long periods away from home to compete internationally after her babies were born.

With birth, neither of my babies descended on to my cervix, and with Charlie my uterus almost ruptured, so both children were born through Caesarean sections which meant a longer recovery time.

With Louisa, I'd been selected for the World Championships which, if I'd had a natural birth, I probably would have been able to compete in, but I had to pull out. I got back to physical work and basic training around six weeks after both were born. With Caesareans you have to let the muscles naturally find their way back together.

I also breastfed both children until they were four. That was trickier with Louisa as she didn't take to expressed milk out of a bottle. So, I had to adapt to two ninety-minute training sessions a day to fit around her. Charlie was much more laid-

back about the bottle, so I could ride for three hours in one go. I think I managed to avoid the mum guilt because everything I was doing was around them eating and getting them to sleep. I'd train when they settled.

Sarah also credits British Cycling with making her path back to competition easier. After she broached the subject, the governing body agreed to adapt the way she worked to suit her new role as a mother.

Following a conversation with British skeleton champion Shelley Rudman, she used the blueprint she'd established with her governing body about how she might juggle her two roles. As a result, Sarah now travels separately and lives separately from other athletes in the camp whenever she is away. Her entourage consists of her husband – fellow cyclist Barney – both her children plus her parents. In fact, she won't travel without them.

Perhaps her emotion at the 2020 Tokyo Paralympics said it all and I'll never forget watching the normally stoic Sarah fight back the tears after winning three golds. Afterwards she admitted she'd found the games one of the most challenging because athletes' families had not been allowed to travel alongside competitors due to Covid-19 restrictions.

You're not an athlete 24/7, but you are a mum 24/7, and when I spoke to British Cycling, I said I wanted to do both. But one of the things I found so hard in Japan was that it wasn't just about me and my wellbeing. I still get twenty questions from Charlie about why I had to disappear for twenty-two days and not just one night. So, the wellbeing of my children also directly impacts the wellbeing of me as an athlete and my ability to deliver.

When you take that holistic approach to making sure that athletes can deliver with no distractions then it works. Because we travel separately, stay separately and I commute in to do my job, there's a bigger logistical pressure on me. But having my children with me makes me a stronger athlete and a more reliable athlete. What I've chosen might not be right for another woman. A female has to be allowed to decide what's right for her and her family, but having that communication opened up that conversation.

Elite men who have families also have different levels of challenge, and that shouldn't be ignored. If Barney had also had to train and compete and hadn't been at home doing all the cooking and cleaning and washing while I was feeding, I couldn't have managed.

Already, Sarah has not ruled out defending her titles at the Paris Paralympics in 2024, nor is there any mention of her retiring. When we speak, she's set her sights on riding the Glasgow World Championships in 2023, competing against the best able-bodied cyclists – races she's tried to gain selection to before but not succeeded. Just as she did when she was a teenager, she is always going one better, pushing the boundaries of her performance and of Paralympian competition. However these days, the motivation that keeps her going is different, she says.

I never imagined that I'd still be training and competing when my children started on their sporting journeys. Louisa is doing swim training now, and I guess it's about wanting to be that role model. In 2022 I had a fairly major crash where I broke two ribs and suffered a partially collapsed lung. It showed me that everything could be taken away from me quickly.

But that enjoyment of sport has been a way of life for me, and while I've still got my health and an ability to keep challenging at the highest level, then I wouldn't want to stop.

Continuing to compete after that crash also became about me setting an example for Louisa and Charlie. By carrying on I was saying to them, you will hit bumps in the road. From the outside everything looks dead smooth. People see the good stuff every four years, especially in Parasport. They don't see half of the things you've done in between Games because the coverage just stops. So the example you provide is to your immediate circle, to the people who can see what's happening. I always say to my kids, 'If we didn't try, we would always wonder.' And even though I'm forty-five I still have to try, because if I didn't I would always wonder.

CHAPTER 5

Strength and Power

Fatima Whitbread MBE

JAVELIN THROWER

'I got offered a scholarship to go to LA and train.
I said no; I didn't want to leave my mum. It
was so much more to me than just a javelin.'

It was in 1979 when a sixteen-year-old Fatima Whitbread beat off a Soviet and German challenge to be crowned the first British winner of a European junior javelin championship in Bydgoszcz in Poland. It was the moment that would be the first step on a sporting journey that would eventually see her take bronze at the 1984 Olympics, break the world record in a qualifying round of the European Athletics Championships in 1986 on the way to winning the gold medal, then win silver at the 1988 Olympics after clinching gold at the World Championships in Rome in 1987.

Yet during that decade when Fatima was reaching her peak, the Cold War between the Soviet bloc and the West was also reaching new heights. The threat of nuclear war was a present danger, and throughout the 1970s and 1980s international sport became another arena where tensions played out and rival powers fought for dominance. It wasn't until the fall of the Berlin Wall in 1989 that a new era of reconciliation was ushered in worldwide. As Fatima tells me when we meet, it was East versus West – a head-to-head battle that she revelled in and also a period, she believes, that defined a unique era in the history of British sport.

The 1980s were a golden age in all sport, but in athletics we had Daley Thompson, Sebastian Coe, Steve Ovett, Steve Cram, there was me and Tessa Sanderson, then a little later came sprinters like Linford Christie and John Regis and hurdle champion Sally Gunnell. There was no end of talent. Athletics was coming out of amateur sport into professionalism. We built that platform and it's been beautiful to see youngsters doing really well in the Golden League (a series of outdoor track-and-field meetings organized by the IAAF and replaced by the Diamond League in 2010). I thoroughly enjoyed every moment of what I did when I did it and I wouldn't want to be in this era. There's a huge expectation and pressure on young people. Many of them get the best of what's available to them, and good luck to them, but it's all done on a very big stage. I liked it when we were competing because we did it despite the system. And it doesn't matter what you're given, if you haven't got passion and drive you won't succeed.

As a sportswoman who has competed worldwide, I understand exactly the pressure and expectation of the modern era that Fatima describes. But I'm also aware that I've enjoyed the benefits of that professionalism Fatima and others laid the foundations for. Given the vast difference in our experience, I was fascinated to understand more about how she fought to become one of the most iconic figures of her generation – her sturdy, muscular physique and her trademark celebratory wiggle defined her. But for me, she was always so much more than a sporting superstar. She was a woman who defied the traditional tall, blonde and slender feminine ideal of beauty that was accepted at the time when she took to the world stage.

I was a burly girl and I was tough physically and mentally. Put those two together and it was a force to be reckoned with. I started training when I was around thirteen. My dad worked in Tilbury Docks, and a docker's life was a tough one. My grandad also worked there and a chap he worked with was a boxer called Micky Malt. He asked Micky if I could train weights with him. He'd kitted out his garden shed and it had bars with railway wheels on the end of them. It was a narrow area so you had to be precise in your movements. We put mirrors up on the ceiling so we could check when we bench-pressed and did snaps, and we did a lot of speed-ball work. It was cold in the

1970s, especially in that shed. It was my passion because there was no way you could do that for twenty years if it wasn't. It was a wonderful opportunity.

But while Fatima's professional battles played out at the track, mainly against her Eastern bloc rivals, her ultimate battle throughout her childhood was with herself. The story of how Fatima even made it to that training shed in Essex is unimaginable to me. Having been born Fatima Vedad in north London to a Turkish Cypriot mother and Greek Cypriot father, her father walked out on the family before she was born. At just three months old she was abandoned again, this time by her mother.

A neighbour heard a baby crying in the flat for two days. She didn't see anyone come or go so she called the police and they rescued me. I got taken into hospital with nappy rash and malnutrition and I was there for six months before Hackney Borough Council made me a ward of court. I was put in a children's home in Harpenden where I stayed for the first five years of my life. It was daunting. You didn't get the hugs and the cuddles and kisses that you needed. All the kids were crying for Mummy or couldn't understand why they were there. It was emotionally traumatic because you could never feel comfortable in your own skin. You were constantly besieged with: 'Where's Mummy?' And I was asking those questions, too. Every car that came into the driveway, I'd ask, 'Is that my mummy coming to get me?' We had to be survivors because if you weren't you would very easily go under.

The first time Fatima met her biological mother in her memory was just before she was relocated to a second care home in Essex at the age of five.

The matron called me and said, 'Fatima, make sure you are downstairs at 9 a.m. Your mother is coming to take you to a new home where your half-brother and sister will be. By then, I didn't think I had a mother. I was worried all night. When the doorbell rang in the morning, I could see this large lady through the opaque glass. As the door opened I got this whoosh of strong perfume and I saw a woman with a gold tooth and big black, bushy hair. My mother never made eye contact once. She didn't pick me up once. It was a long journey down to Essex and I was looking out of the car window crying, wondering what was going to happen to me. In the new home there were fourteen kids, and when I went into the garden a little girl ran up and said, 'You must be my half-sister. Come with me.' The kids were playing on the climbing frame, and a lad came along and said, 'You're my half-sister.' Suddenly I felt a hand across my chest. It was my mother. She said, 'You behave yourself and look after them or I'll cut your throat.' Then she started to talk to them in her Turkish mother tongue. My half-siblings understood her but I didn't understand a word.

Within two weeks she was back to take them and she feigned that she wanted to take me too. I didn't want to go but the matrons told me that I should try to integrate. When we got to the bus stop she pulled out a ten bob note from her bag, poked me in the ribs and said, 'We don't want you. We don't love you.' In my head, I was going with her to be in a family, but she sent me back to the home, except it wasn't my home because it was full of strangers.

Given the heartbreak and instability of Fatima's early years, I was interested to know whether sport was ever encouraged while she lived in the care homes or became a focus for her during that traumatic time.

I used to play football in the garden with the boys and climb trees and we used to go apple scrumping a lot. And we'd throw stones at each other in the park. Our bikes in the children's homes were donated by families around us, mainly because they didn't work properly. But we fixed the tyres and the brakes and rode them too. That was my focus and my challenge, but I was a rascal. I was a tomboy into rough and tumble and rolling my sleeves up. My socks would be around my ankles and I'd be covered in mud.

In fact, it wasn't until Fatima got to school that she ever participated in organized sport, and similar to many children that I've talked to from disadvantaged backgrounds, she quickly discovered a talent that may never have been recognized had the focus remained on her to achieve academically.

Sport became my saviour. I was in all the teams. I was pretty good at hockey and netball and other kids didn't like it because I was a first year knocking out the senior teams. I was sturdy, but I wasn't a fit little kid because I was living on beans on toast and sugar sandwiches and I never wanted to get in the free school-dinner line because we got the piss taken out of us.

I used to say to my mate Alma who lived in a care home around the corner, 'I'll earn us our dinner money so we don't have to stand in line.' I often got a penny from the headmaster because he would send me on errands. I was always outside his office because I couldn't concentrate. I was too disturbed. So, he'd ask me to go to the corner shop and buy him cigarettes and he'd give me a penny. And that's when I could go round the back of the bike sheds to play penny up the wall – closest to the wall takes all. And I did very well. But if I didn't have enough I went to the corner shop and bought us a carrot. Or I'd go to the fish and chip shop and ask for scraps. Back then people were kind and they'd throw you a few chips.

Soon, I realized that wasn't good enough. I wanted to earn respect from my peers, and to try and feel good about myself and have a bit of confidence. When it came to studies I was imprisoned in my own head. But when I played sport I forgot about all the problems I had. For me, it was about finding something that I could feel an affinity with.

But what was sport like for girls in the 1970s? Fatima explains that it was not taken that seriously even though she rose to lead both her hockey and netball teams. Had it not been for a chance meeting with a female coach called Margaret Whitbread, her life may have been very different. Nearing her teenage years, she'd suffered an even worse cruelty. After a brief and horrific stay back with her birth mother, she'd been raped at knifepoint by her mother's drunken boyfriend. Fatima was only twelve years old. At school her behaviour became so bad that a child psychologist was brought in who stopped her from seeing her mother again. But it was Margaret and the javelin who were to truly save Fatima.

I was around thirteen when two school teams were playing netball in the league. I was trying to get my team to focus but the whistle blew and this voice said, 'Young lady. Any more noise and you'll be off.' I thought, who is this woman talking to me like this when I'm trying to motivate my team? I carried on, and thankfully we won.

At the end of the game I said to Alma, 'Let's go to the athletics club.' It was the end of the season and I hated it when I didn't have any focus through sport. We walked the five miles to the track, Alma joined the sprinters and I saw this tall boy called Jack throwing what I thought was a spear. I went to pick it up but he said, 'Young lady, you can't do that. You'll have to wait for the javelin coach.' I sat in the stand toe-tapping until I saw this person walking towards me. As she got closer, I thought, it's that same bloody woman. I was worried because I thought she was going to give me a mouthful. Jack told her I wanted to throw the javelin but before he could introduce me, she said, 'I know who you are. You're Fatima, aren't you? Let me tell you, young lady. I won't be having any of that cheek you gave on the netball court.' I promised to behave if she gave me a go.

As the weeks went by she said I had some talent and asked for my mum and dad to come up. After asking me several times she thought there was something wrong with my hearing. She said to Jack, 'I keep asking Fatima if she'll bring her mum and dad up to talk about getting her some kit.' That's when he told her I lived in the children's homes. The next week she threw some boots down and said, 'They're size seven. They're probably too big for you but stuff them with paper.' And she gave me an old-school javelin that was green and rattled. I loved it. No one had ever given me anything. When I got home that evening I was showing my friend Ingrid how to throw it in the back garden and it went smash, right through the French windows. I got a month's ban and had to come straight home every evening after school. But a message got back to me from the netball team saying, 'Mrs Whitbread thinks you've bunked off and sold the boots and the javelin.' That night, I got up at 2 a.m. and wrote her a letter saying that I couldn't come to the track because I'd smashed the windows but that I wanted to be the best javelin thrower. When Mrs Whitbread came over she must have been quite persistent because a week later I was back at the track.

As time went on, Margaret invited Fatima to have tea at her house and meet her husband and two sons. Then she spent a couple of weeks with her during the holidays. The adjustment took time for both of them, Fatima says, but eventually Margaret asked her if she wanted to live with her permanently.

When she asked me if I wanted to become a Whitbread and change my name I said, 'If I become a Whitbread then you'll be my mum.' And, as time went on, I stopped calling her Mrs Whitbread and I called her Mum, and my dad, Dad. To my younger brothers I was always known as 'big sis'. I didn't stick with javelin for the sport itself. It was because I'd been adopted into the Whitbread family. Not long after, I got offered a scholarship to go to LA and train as an athlete. Later, I was also offered a career in golf. It was £60,000 a year but I said no; I didn't want to leave my mum. It was so much more to me than just a javelin.

By the time Fatima began training in the shed, she'd already set her sights on the Olympics. Inspired by the pentathlete and shot-putter Mary Peters whom she'd seen on TV competing at the 1972 Munich Olympics, she figured she needed to bulk up to become a world-beating thrower. As someone who's trained with weights myself and, as a result, felt embarrassed and self-conscious about my body image, I wondered how Fatima viewed her changing physique and dealt with the often disparaging comments she received from the outset of her career?

I knew that I needed to beef up to be the best in the world so
that's what I did. With training I could see my body changing
all the time. I had no nutritionist but I needed to bulk up to
get the power in my arms. I couldn't eat junk because it was
fat, so I drank protein drinks: milk with banana and Complan
drinks with three raw eggs – 8,000 calories a day. It used to
make me gag.

But the perception of me as a strong woman was terrible.
I'm not sure I dealt with the silly comments like 'You're like
a man because you've got muscles' very well. But for me, the
urge to be successful outweighed everything. And I didn't want
to waste my energy arguing with people because, as it turned
out, there were a lot of people who thought I was sexy and
would try and hit on me as well – both men and women. I
got on with it. I loved doing what I did and I wanted to be
the best.

When I trained I also had access to a support team which included
technicians, nutritionists, psychologists and physiotherapists,
as all modern-era athletes do. But with none of that available
to Fatima, I wanted to understand how she learned to perfect
her run-up and throw, given that javelin balances athletic speed
with technique and strength.

Mum and I would talk about my training. We agreed that I
needed to be fast and I needed to be fit. So I'd be running, doing
weights, and then I'd have my biometric work where I'd jump

up and down on boxes with my left then right leg. Hurdles were for hips. I did it all through watching others.

Biomechanics to me was all about putting a VHS tape in the machine and recording. I recorded Marlies Göhr, who was an East German sprinter, to find out how to get my legs to move quicker. I looked at the East German throwers image by image then broke it down stage by stage to see how they moved and how they worked at their optimum best to try to incorporate some of that into what I was doing technically. You had to use your own initiative to do your homework. Nowadays you can do all that in a heartbeat on a computer, but I took painstaking time to work out the best way for me to be 100 per cent on the runway without a millimetre being out of place or any time lost. From start to finish it was all about upper strength and power, elasticity and then explosiveness at the end.

Once Fatima started competing on a world stage, she also trained with athletes from a variety of disciplines, learning enough technique from each to incorporate it into her own programme. Nowadays, athletes are far more spoon-fed with training programmes mapped out for them, but listening to her regime, it's the level of self-discipline that she had that I find the most astounding.

I watched the foreign world record holders when they came over from places like East Germany. I would sneak out the back of competitions and watch their training sessions and I learned a lot. Eventually I also went to the sprint group. I didn't want to train to the same intensity because I didn't want to be an 800-metre runner, but I'd talk with the coach and say I needed to be strong and fast and I trained with both men and women. I took a little bit from all their programmes. I was training with runners like Verona Elder and the decathlete Daley Thompson. I was their hare. I got a two-metre start and they'd have to catch me and run me down. When it came to my bounding, I went to Willie Banks, who was the USA triple jump world record holder and I asked him to help me write a programme. And I learned from the weightlifter Precious McKenzie and the shot-putter Geoff Capes. I took a little bit from everybody and went down the middle.

I wrote it all down on a daily basis: my training, my preparation, how to peak for the competitions and how to peak for the championships. I'd know what my competition programme was and where my improvements were needed, and I'd know how to get to certain levels at different times of the year.

It's also Fatima's persistence that marks her out as a true champion for me. It took her twelve long years to gain that first junior title in 1979, and for the next decade she fought against rivals from Finland's Tina Lilak to Britain's Tessa Sanderson, to the East German Petra Felke to win her major titles, a competitor whom she fought with on the runway but whom she was the best of friends with off the track. Of those women, the British press built up her rivalry with Tessa Sanderson into one of the bitterest stand-offs in elite women's sport. Sanderson did beat Fatima match for match, but couldn't ever get close to Fatima's fifty-three throws at over 70 metres. I wondered how important rivalry was to Fatima's performance and how much of that rivalry with Sanderson was real or hyped up?

Tessa was five years older than me, and as a youngster coming into international sport, Tessa was my idol. I watched her break the British record. She was an inspiration, but my first meeting with her was when I was around sixteen. I'd been getting some good press as the new kid on the block, but when I met her she told me, 'I didn't train my ass off to be beaten by you.' I kind of got it, but I also didn't. She never warmed to me, but I was determined then that I was going to show her I could be a good thrower.

I also learned that head-to-heads were important and I revelled in them, but it wasn't long before I started to beat Tessa and go up a notch and Felke became my rival. At my top end we were 11 metres ahead of the field, and Tessa finished 11 metres behind us in the Europeans in 1987.

But I was mindful about young girls coming up behind me. I had the time to speak to them and talk to them about training and I tried to inspire them. If they are going to beat you, they will anyway, so at least try and embrace it. So it was a sad affair because the media made a big deal of it as Whitbread vs Sanderson as if we were not good friends, but it was simply that she didn't want to communicate, and I had to respect that.

What was a shame was that when athletics was coming out of amateurism into professionalism, we had what were called medal tariffs, and I believed that a gold medal man and a gold medal woman should be paid the same tariff, and also for silver and bronze. I rang her and said, 'We're a force together so we need to work together to make this happen for women.' But she couldn't and I feel that was detrimental. She and I lost out on what could have been a good rivalry and a good friendship.

But going into the Seoul Olympics in 1988, it wasn't sporting rivalry that threatened to destabilize Fatima's gold medal-winning chances. Instead, it was her traumatic past resurfacing that became her biggest struggle. After breaking the world record with a throw of 77.44 metres in the qualifying round of the 1986 European Championships, then in 1987 winning Sports Personality of the Year against a roster of men – one accolade among many others she remains very proud of – the increased public interest in her was to have disastrous consequences.

When you are climbing no one expects anything, only yourself, but when you are the champion then your family and friends and the press and the public have expectations. You go to the shops to buy something and people come up to you. Back in the day they wanted autographs and I always carried around a wad of pictures in my bag. I wanted to give people the time.

But the tabloid press thought it was all right to go to my biological mother's house. They took with them a picture of me in a frame and photographed her holding it saying she wanted her blood-daughter back. My husband at the time said now I was champion my story needed to be told, and either I had to tell it or the press would do what they wanted. I didn't want to do it. I was very protective about my adoptive family and my mum got very upset because she didn't know if I was going to leave the family. I told her, 'Don't be silly. You're my mum.'

I wrote a book in 1987. I'd just come off a big sporting year and with success comes responsibility. I was quite a shy person and now I had all these after-dinner speeches and award ceremonies to go to. I found it all very stressful. Plus I was unearthing things about my past that I'd buried. It ran like a movie through my head. I had a terrible breakdown physically and mentally. I remember I had heel trouble and a doctor gave me an injection. I felt this terrible pain, and from that day on I was never the same again. It tipped me over the edge from being organized and capable to being tired and feeling like I was walking on cobblestones all the time. Anyone who's had a breakdown will understand it's like a slow-lifting fog.

It happened in the winter period and I was trying to train for the Seoul Olympics. I shouldn't really have gone to the Olympics. I'd lost all concentration and perception of time. But I gave myself a talking-to and said, I can do this. I ended up with a silver which, given where I'd come from, I was not ashamed of.

Eventually Fatima was forced to officially retire in 1992, but only after a botched shoulder operation to resolve an injury she dates back to her 1986 world-record-breaking throw left her with severed nerves. Back then keyhole surgery was not widely available and Fatima paid the price. Hearing her story also highlights to me just how much strides in medical science as well as technology have helped to change sport in the intervening years. Yet, for women, some aspects of the elite competition have been far slower to shift.

Battle lines are still drawn around equality of pay and prize money for women. In tennis, thanks to the tireless campaigning of women like former US tennis star Billie Jean King, equal prize money exists across all four major championships. More sports have followed suit, but others such as football, golf and basketball still lag behind. Equal pay is yet to be achieved in most of women's sports. Of the 100 highest paid sportspeople worldwide, only two women – US tennis stars Serena Williams and Naomi Osaka – make the list.

Women in sport are also being faced with new and more complex issues. Inclusion in the women's category of women who have transitioned from being biologically male to female is proving controversial for many of sport's governing bodies where decision now lies. For me, abuse of any transgender person at any level of sport must be called out, but an open discussion must also be allowed to continue around safety and fairness when it comes to elite competition. Given that Fatima herself found sport because she was included, I was interested to hear her views on transgender inclusion at the elite women's level – a subject that is far more likely to generate articles today than in her era. Does she support inclusion at all costs or want to balance it with fairness based on current available scientific evidence – a viewpoint that I and others such as former British swimmer Sharron Davies and runner Paula Radcliffe also share?

It's scientifically proven that once men have gone through puberty they remain in a male body in terms of strength. A man's frame is different and there's a massive advantage for them. Women have trained very hard to try to achieve something and this shouldn't be thrown into the equation for them. When I trained with men, I was never going to beat them. When I practised with the sprint group and we did staggered starts at the track and I was used as the hare, it was the men's goal to close the gap, and they always did.

For me, it is not at all ridiculous that transgender people should want to be included, but it is ridiculous that trans women who have gone through male puberty should compete against women. I do think transgender people should have their own category, and [given the amount of airspace this is taking up] *this needs to be dealt with and it needs to be dealt with fast.*

While the transgender issue undoubtedly attracts emotive headlines, it must also be seen in proportion. Since the Olympic committee issued its first transgender policy in 2003, two transgender women athletes [out of a total of over 71,000 people competing to qualify] have reached an Olympics, including trans woman Laurel Hubbard who competed in the weightlifting category at Tokyo 2020. However, others identifying as trans or non-binary, such as the Canadian soccer star Quinn who is non-binary but who competes in the women's category in line with Quinn's birth sex, have competed in greater numbers over the years. While important, the subject of inclusion, Fatima stresses, must stretch far wider than just gender. As a regular visitor to schools, she understands how the Covid-19 pandemic has restricted access to sport for so many people, especially children from low socio-economic and disadvantaged backgrounds similar to hers.

The sad fact is that in the present day teenage girls often drop out of sport when they hit puberty because of fear of judgement, lack of confidence and lack of opportunity. Add to that the pressures on those girls from underserved communities who may be required to help out more at home, are unable to travel to a club due to cost, or avoid competing altogether due to issues such as period poverty, then the problem becomes even more acute. Fatima herself competed at a time when there was no funding, juggling a part-time job as a fitness instructor and helping out at home with her two younger brothers while training in the mornings and evenings.

Access to free sports facilities can also hold many girls back. Fatima became one of the first athletes to speak out about the mass sell-off of school playing fields which began in the 1980s and which has continued to today albeit at lesser rates. For all the pressure and expectation of the big stage of the modern-day era, catching children like her and giving them an opportunity to try sport must start at school, she says.

I was livid when lots of playing fields got sold off because you are taking away all these opportunities, especially for kids who live in high-rise flats. It's madness. Sport starts at school. Sport was my saviour and I think kids need to be offered a lot more understanding that sport is a lifestyle. Take the time to talk to kids about diet and movement and as they grow older they will stay in that mindset. It's not about being a world champion, it's about getting out and kicking a ball around. We need to invest time in them as people. Then, if they want to take it to club level, or international level, they'll get the bit between their teeth and want to do that. But you have to get them to bite.

My journey has not just been about the medals, it's been about learning who I am. It's been about learning to cope with failure. Failure is about taking something away from that competition and improving yourself. For me it's been magnificent. The medals are nice, but the experience is the greatest I've ever had.

CHAPTER 6

In the Moment

Sky Brown

SKATEBOARDER

'If people say, "What's she doing? Girls can't skate!" I don't say anything. I just let my skateboarding do the talking.'

Sky Brown is on top of the world. The fourteen-year-old has just returned from the World Skate Championships in Sharjah in the United Arab Emirates after being crowned Great Britain's first skateboarding world champion. After three gravity-defying runs she finished four points ahead of her rival Japan's Kokona Hiraki and five points ahead of her best friend Sakura Yosozumi. Brown is the British-Japanese teenager who, in 2021, became Great Britain's youngest Olympian of all time and, consequently, the nation's youngest medallist. Her enthusiasm is infectious. As the superstar of the social media generation, she oozes super-cool. Yet underneath her sunny smile is one determined girl.

Being world champion is pretty crazy. I was so stoked to win. It was so much fun being in Sharjah, being back with everyone and getting back on the podium with Sakura was cool too.
I think having the Olympics behind me really helped and it was crazy to see how everyone has grown so much since then and there are so many new skaters. The sport is really growing and there's a lot of new tricks, so I just want to keep skating, keep pushing and keep getting better.
On my last run, I actually went the wrong way. It's why I was so stoked to get that win because I hadn't actually practised that last bit. But skating is like a dance. If you mess up you can get back to where you were.

For a team athlete like me, used to a high level of prescriptive play and also strict rules around what to wear, I'll admit to feeling a little envious of a sport where there are so few rules. With its heelflips, kickflips, mid-air spins and ollies (jumps), creativity is at the heart of skateboarding. Competitors must only complete their timed runs without using any supports for balance and each run is scored on its technical aspects from how the skater uses the course, to their consistency, style and speed. It makes skaters the architects of their own destiny – from the tricks they pick to the outfits they wear. Sky calls the skatepark her playground where there are seemingly no limits to where her imagination can take her.

The cool thing about skateboarding is that when you're in the bowl (bowl skating evolved from the culture of underground skating in disused swimming pools during a severe drought in California in the late 1970s) you're just skating. You forget about everything else that's going on. You forget all about the crowd. It's just you and your run. It's like a dance routine that we all do in succession and that's why I think we're all pretty chill on the skateboard. You're just in the moment.

For Sky, being in that moment is a labour of love. Since the age of three she's had a skateboard in her hand. She was born to a Japanese mother Mieko and English dad Stewart, a skater himself who has also been her primary tutor. Sky grew up in Miyazaki in Japan and now splits her time between Japan and Orange County on the California coast. But was it always a foregone conclusion that Sky would follow in the family footsteps?

We had a backyard mini ramp that my dad built and he skated on it with his friends. I remember watching him when I was young and I just loved the way skateboarding looked. It looked so beautiful and so cool and I just thought, 'I want to do that.'

Before I got my first skateboard, I practised on my dad's and it was my favourite toy. I was riding it everywhere. I loved it and I didn't want to stop. Then, when I was six years old I got my first skateboard. The graphic on the board was a bunch of stiletto heels and make-up painted on it. It was really girly and I loved it. I love getting dirty, but you have to have some fun too, so I'm also a girly girl.

But I grew up in a small town in Japan and a lot of the girls there stayed inside a lot. The girls were scared to go outside because there were so many boys. But I was always outside learning how to skate and getting dirty. So, since I was little I've always wanted to inspire girls.

Yet being a female skater, even in Sky's generation, has been a slow revolution. Up until recently the sport, which women began competing in during the 1960s, remained a traditionally male subculture broken through only by a handful of pioneers. In 1965 Californian teenager Patti McGee became the first female champion at the National Skateboard Championships. In the 1970s Peggy Oki, who grew up in California and who began skateboarding when she was ten, went on to become the only female member of a competition team of skaters known as the Z-Boys.

A decade later, names such as Anita Tessensohn and Leaf Treinen became the faces of female skateboarding, both appearing in American skateboard company Powell-Peralta's iconic advertising campaign: 'Some girls play with dolls. Real women skate'. However, due to the sport's perceived danger it has gone through peaks and troughs with the closure of skateparks at times forcing it back to its underground roots.

Sky has several role models, she tells me, but even after 2015 when she first progressed from the backyard ramp on to the skateparks, she was in a minority.

I had people I looked up to and I've always loved people who had beautiful style in skateboarding. Christian Hosoi and Greyson Fletcher are skaters I've always loved. And the girl I looked up to is the street skater Leticia Bufoni. I remember watching her videos and I felt really inspired by her. I watched her fall down so hard and get back up and she was always pushing so hard. She was a great role model for me.

But the first time I went to the skatepark it was a bit scary. There weren't many girls there, only big guys who were flying around everywhere, but I just wanted to get out there and play too. Sometimes when I was there, or if I posted anything online, there were people who said, 'What's she doing? Girls can't skate!' I didn't say anything. I just let my skateboarding do the talking. Whenever I heard that I just felt more pumped up and ready to go out there and prove them wrong.

But there were also boys who helped me. When you go to the skatepark it's like one big family. People were giving me tips or telling me to try a trick or showing me something cool if I asked them how to do it. So you meet friends and they teach you stuff. Skateboarding is all about taking small steps. You can't just go from an ollie to skating on a mega ramp. You have to learn step by step. But my dad is the one that really helped me and he taught me lots of tricks.

As a member of the presenting team during the Tokyo Olympics, I remember being glued to the skateboarding events, not just to experience the thrill of watching skaters fly through the air but because of the unique skate culture around the competition. Although skating is a highly individual sport, the family spirit that Sky describes, especially among her fellow competitors, is as strong as in any winning team. If a competitor falls during their run, everyone is there to help. Everyone applauds each other's runs. Her best friend Sakura is also one of her fiercest rivals, yet Sky sees the ethos of sharing and learning as the only way the sport grows in popularity and progresses in technique – a freedom and growth mindset rarely expressed in more traditional sports.

Skateboarding is a big family and we need each other to keep pushing and we need each other to get better and to grow. It's definitely weird competing against people who are your best friends, but the way I think of it is that sometimes you're going to lose and sometimes you are going to win. You can fall on any little trick and so we all need each other.

When we started there weren't so many girls skating so we stuck together. Sakura and I have known each other since I was seven. We're best friends and we've pretty much grown up together. We know each other's tricks and each other's moves. Sometimes people will keep their new tricks a secret but most of the time they will bring them out in practice. And when Sakura and I practise together we really try to help each other's run.

We also really want to beat each other, but when Sakura beats me I'm just so stoked for her and she feels the same when I win.

Sky makes her sport look like an art form, yet many of her tricks are learned from watching YouTube videos of other skaters. She was the first ever girl to land a 720, one of the rarest tricks in skateboarding with two full mid-air rotations. But none of that comes easily. And while Sky doesn't talk about 'training' – instead, she calls it practising and having fun – that practice is relentless. Any competition run is a well-rehearsed sequence of moves that I confess I would be rubbish at remembering, let alone perfecting. Yet 'messing up' is also a crucial part of the skater's journey.

Developing the confidence to bring yourself back to your routine after making a mistake is something that even as an experienced hockey player I struggled with. If I ever did mess up on the pitch it took the efforts of a sports psychologist to get me back on track. I also replayed videos of myself making winning passes and tackles to help reprogram my mind. But with no formal coaching team behind her and no psychologist, I find Sky's resilience nothing short of remarkable.

A run is exactly like a dance. I've run through it so much and you really have to practise it a lot. To have the routine locked in you're just repeating it over and over. After that you know what you're doing most of the time.

But on a skateboard it's really easy to mess up, but whatever you do you have to put in 100 per cent commitment to it. So, when I'm doing a trick like a kickflip – when I have to use my feet to spin the board and land back on it – it's a really risky trick. A lot of the time you don't know if you're going to fall or if you're going to make it. You just have to commit and see what happens. When you do mess up, you do get nervous for the next one, but you just have to keep pushing. Skating makes you brave and strong.

When I competed in the Olympics I fell on my trick twice. It was a kickflip and it's a risky trick. When I did the safety run I didn't pull out that trick but when it came to the full run, I was just so hyped I just wanted to do a kickflip. But I fell and it was scary. After my second time, I thought, 'Oh my goodness! I haven't fallen that much in practice. This is weird.' But as soon as I came off, I spoke to my dad and to Sakura. My dad said, 'It's okay, don't worry. The cops aren't going to fine you for messing up.' And Sakura also told me it was okay. After that I felt better and it was okay.

With such a wise head on young shoulders, it's easy to forget that Sky is still only fourteen years old and hasn't even taken her high school diploma yet. Yet she's smashing it both on and off the skatepark. She turned professional aged nine and won a lucrative and ongoing sponsorship deal with Nike two years later, becoming the company's youngest sponsored athlete. She has 1.3 million followers on Instagram and 2.1 million on

TikTok, making her a skateboarding icon and a style icon too. She now spends much of her time travelling the world, but she still has to fit school work around her sport, as well as simply enjoying being a teenager. Was devoting her life to skating so early a difficult choice, I wondered?

It wasn't a tough decision at all. I knew skateboarding was what I wanted to do forever, but when I was younger I didn't think about competing in it, or anything like the Olympics. It just felt like a playground.

When I started competing I had to fit school work in around it, but it's honestly pretty easy. Most days, I'll surf first thing, come back, do some school and then I'll go and skate or I'll go back to the ocean. The day is pretty long and I wake up pretty early – maybe 5.30 a.m. – so I can fit a lot in.

I have a school tutor twice a week and my mum is my Japanese teacher so she keeps me on top of it because Japanese is hard. I'm travelling all the time, but I've been travelling since I was little and I love travelling. And when I am travelling, fitting in school is just as easy because I can do it online. I have a good routine at home, but I can adapt it when I'm away.

When it comes to keeping a healthy routine, my mum is a nutritionist so she always makes breakfast, lunch and dinner. We rarely eat out. Sometimes when I go to a competition we'll get a place with a kitchen and Mum cooks and always makes sure I'm eating healthily, giving me the best food and the yummiest food. I'm basically a normal kid. I just do sports.

Did I also forget to mention that Sky is a champion dancer – she won the US version of *Dancing with the Stars: Juniors* when she was ten years old – and an excellent surfer too? In fact, in the run-up to the Tokyo Olympics it was a tough call as to whether she would skateboard or surf in the Summer Games. In the end she chose skateboarding and opted to compete for Team GB, feeling that Skateboard GB [the British skateboarding association] had a more relaxed approach than its Japanese equivalent.

However, the two disciplines share the same creative ethos and are closely intertwined, the modern skateboard being invented in the 1950s because surfers wanted a sport to take part in when the waves were low.

And both sports share techniques and tricks. Skating and surfing need good balance on the board. When it comes to generating speed, skaters tic-tac – a side-to-side shoulder movement that shifts weight on to the hips and allows their feet to move the board from left to right or vice versa to gain momentum. In surfing a similar move is called pumping. And when it comes to turning or directing the board, the movement in both sports also comes from the hips. But it's not only Sky's technical ability in skating that has marked her out as world class; it's also her ability to make it look stylish, something she says comes from alternating between surfing and skating.

Surfing and skateboarding are pretty similar and one helps me with the other. I think I get a little bit of my style from surfing and I get my airs (aerial tricks where skaters ride all four wheels off the ground) from skateboarding. A lot of how I use my arms and legs works in both – and the tricks are very similar.

How many hours I spend surfing a day can depend on the waves. Sometimes the waves can be so bad, but on other days they can be so fiery. I can stay out there for five or six hours if the waves are pumping, but if it's windy and crazy then I can manage around 30 minutes and I'll go to the skatepark.

My favourite tricks change all the time because I'm always learning new tricks and I figure out new ways to do things and how to add that little bit of extra style. But my favourite skateboarding trick at the moment is a Japan Air – you go high in the air and you hold the board and tweak the move by arching your back. You make it look as beautiful as you can.

Also similar between the two sports are the risks. In worst-case scenarios, coming off your board – a wipeout in surf-speak – can cause severe injury or even death. Skateboarding falls are equally dangerous, and while Sky falls a lot in practice and mostly uses knee and elbow protectors, wrist guards and a helmet to protect her, injuries are an occupational hazard.

Yet Sky has also shown herself to be fearless. In 2019 she competed in the Dew Tour (an extreme sports contest) which doubled as her first Olympics qualifier with her arm in a bright pink cast, having broken it in an accident only weeks before. Another far more devastating fall in 2020 in the run-up to the Tokyo Olympics almost took her life. Beforehand, she'd rarely spoken about her accidents, saying she always wants people to see the fun in what she does, but on this occasion she went public. Even now watching the footage back is terrifying, and being a mum myself I can only imagine the trauma her parents had to go through. Sky was around 15 feet in the air when she fell in the eight-foot gap between two vertical ramps plummeting head-first on to a concrete floor. She was unconscious for around twelve hours and suffered a fractured skull and wrist. She also sustained lacerations to her heart, lungs and stomach, smashed up two fingers and a cracked front tooth.

I don't remember too much about that fall, but I do remember grabbing on to this wooden ledge in the gap and that helped my landing go a little slower so I saved it well. My arm was also around my head and I was wearing a good helmet. But I was really lucky. If I didn't have my arm there and I didn't have my helmet it could have been way worse.

My dad was there and he was filming me, and my younger brother, Ocean, was also there and he was skating behind the gap so he saw everything too. It was pretty scary for them. My mum was outside asleep in the car and so she was really shocked when she heard the helicopters land and the ambulance sirens. It definitely woke her up!

At the hospital, for those first few hours, it was touch and go whether Sky would survive, the experience for her and her family made all the worse by Covid-19 restrictions limiting visitors to her bedside. When she did come around, was there a big part of her that never wanted to go near a skateboard again?

It was hard in the hospital. I couldn't see my brother the whole time. And only one member of my family was allowed in at any one time, so my mum and dad had to take it in turns. I had no real memory of what had happened, but when I came round I saw my mum crying next to me, but I didn't want anyone to feel bad.

Everyone took really good care of me and my parents brought me all my favourite food like ramen and lots of traditional Japanese food. They also brought me great nail polish. The hospital also looked after me so well and I'm really grateful.

The whole time I was in hospital I had no doubt that I would skateboard again. As soon as I was healed I was determined to get back on ... and also to get back to the ocean. But my parents did not want me to at all. They said, 'Please don't, Sky. Go dancing. Anything but skateboarding.' And I did go and do some dance classes, but I always knew I was going to be skateboarding again. I didn't want to give up because I didn't want anything to beat me. My full recovery took around two months and the doctor said he was amazed at how quickly I recovered.

Now, I don't want to think of that fall as a real down moment, but it was pretty bad. But I honestly don't think I'd be here today if I didn't have that experience. It's made me so much stronger.

Wow. All I can say is Sky is one tough cookie. But I was also interested in why she decided to share the full details of the fall with her million-plus social media following.

I put a video online about it because on social media we always show the good side of things. Everyone thinks everything is perfect and that maybe I'm a super-girl. Because we always try to show the positive stuff I felt I needed to say, 'We're going to fall, we're going to slam sometimes. It's not always positive but that's life. I'm going to get back up and keep going because that's what happens and if you skateboard you're going to fall sometimes.'

Sky didn't just make a full recovery. Four months later she became the first female to ride the mega ramp built by professional skateboarder Elliot Sloan at his home in Vista in California. Sloan's mega park, which was completed in 2020 and took three years to build, is now one of the most iconic on the skateboarding circuit and features a 100-foot vertical ramp with an 18-foot gap between two half-pipes. That day she was joined by the legendary skateboarder 54-year-old Tony Hawk, whom Sky often trains with and who has described her as 'one of the best female skaters ever, if not one of the best well-rounded skaters ever, regardless of gender'.

But how did Sky go from that horrendous fall to overcoming her fears? After any injury it takes time to come back stronger. I remember during the Champions Trophy in 2014 I cracked two ribs after a rough tackle. When I got back to form, I found myself flinching in my first few games whenever I ran into an opponent, terrified of it happening again. Were there any techniques that Sky used to get her body and mind back to a winning position?

The first time I got back on the skateboard it was on the flat. I just went outside in my backyard and did some basic kerb tricks and some ollies. I took it really slow. I took baby steps. I didn't go straight back into airs, but it felt really good to get back and do some little tricks. In my mind, I just kept trying to focus on what I was going to do next, and that really helped me because then all I felt was excited to get back to skateboarding. Dancing really helped me, too. When I took some dance classes I was moving a lot, trying lots of different styles like hip hop and contemporary. I love dancing and it got me expressing myself again.

But when it came to dropping on the mega ramp, I was excited and nervous and scared. I just wanted to make it. My mum was there to give me a big hug and my dad was there too and my brother. Tony talked me through it. He said as soon as I was in the air, I'd know that I would clear the gap. He said, 'You got it, Sky. Have confidence.' I was scared at the top but I just breathed and prepared myself until I was ready. The first time I skated I cleared the gap, although I came down on my knees on the other side, but soon I was doing straight airs. After the second run it wasn't so scary. It felt great and it was so much fun.

Less than a year later, Sky was competing in the Tokyo Olympics – the first time skateboarding had ever featured in the Olympic line-up, alongside three other new sports: surfing, karate and climbing. With no age limit in the skateboarding category, eighty athletes ranging in age from twelve to forty-six took part in one of two disciplines: park and street, the former being performed in the bowl and the latter when skaters perform tricks over rails, ledges, staircases and other 'street' obstacles. As far as the women's event played out, it was teens like Sky who blazed a trail and showcased a new generation of talent.

At thirteen years old, Sky came away with a bronze medal, completing a flawless final run after two falls in her first and second. But it was also that unique skate culture: the support that the skaters gave each other that marked its Olympic debut as a breath of fresh air. Sky looked completely at home hanging out with her friends, cheering on her friend Sakura as she took the gold, and congratulating then twelve-year-old Kokona Hiraki on her silver.

When I heard that skateboarding was in the Olympics I thought, 'Wow, it would be so cool to get a medal,' and especially as it was the first Olympics that featured skating. So, I was pretty keen on getting it.

My first Olympics was amazing. It was great to be back in my home country and in Tokyo and eating all the Japanese food that I really miss. It was very cool seeing all different kinds of sports people – all different sizes. I saw a really tall basketball player and there were so many ripped people. I had no idea what it was going to be like so I just joined in with everything. I wasn't nervous because being there with all my friends was really cool.

But when I got a medal I had to pinch myself. It felt unreal, like a dream. I knew lots of people around the world would be watching and I knew that it would inspire other girls.

I'm definitely going for Paris 2024, but I'm going to try and surf and skateboard. It's going to be tough, but I'm going to try my best.

Not only has Sky inspired other girls to take up skateboarding, but she's also touched others in so many ways. One of her enduring memories is of going to Cambodia with the project Skateistan who use skateboarding and education to empower children. The project is supported by the Laureus Foundation which uses the power of sport to combat violence against women and girls and tackle gender discrimination. Skateistan works with around 2,500 children, 50 per cent of whom are girls, in places like Afghanistan, Cambodia and South Africa. Sky has not only remained an ambassador for the project, but during the pandemic also took part in an Instagram Live lesson with Tony Hawk to teach children remotely. To raise money for the charity's skate schools she's designed three skateboarding decks with the design company Almost Skateboards, with a percentage of the proceeds being donated to the schools.

When I went to Cambodia and taught kids how to skate, I loved it and it's something I want to do much more of in the future. I love teaching people. And when I went there I learned so much. Kids like me are happy, we have food and we have clean water, but there they didn't have all that stuff. Instead of school, the girls help their mums work, and that made me sad and I wanted to help.

In underprivileged places, skating makes a real difference because when you skate you forget about what you're going through. You're just focused on learning the trick. They'd never seen a skateboard before and so just to show them skateboarding was a really cool thing. I taught them a few tricks. They figured them out pretty fast so we could practise and roll around. And when they got it I saw the biggest smile on their faces. They loved it so much and they had so much fun. Skating made them so happy so I wanted to keep doing that.

And when I designed the boards with Almost I wanted to use a dove as the main graphic because it means peace and kindness.

Seemingly there's no end to Sky's talents, yet despite all her medals and her relentless desire to grow her sport and improve herself, she says that having a platform, whether it's on the world's skateparks or on social media, has allowed her to do the one thing she set out to do: inspire girls. Even as a thirty-something hockey player, I found it impossible not to come away from our conversation feeling inspired. She's not only a role model for her generation, but for every woman regardless of age. We can all learn from her.

Since I was little I've always wanted to inspire girls and get them out there having fun. Sometimes I don't think girls have that freedom. Having the platform of social media has really helped me to have that voice to keep pushing and keep inspiring. I want to show girls that they can do whatever they want. It doesn't matter how old they are, they can do anything.

There are people who have said to me that I do really inspire them and when I hear that it makes me want to go harder for them. When it comes to skateboarding, I get a lot more girls contacting me now because they see me and feel they can try the sport. They can do the same as boys. I want to show that if you believe in yourself you can do it. I hope I've shown that.

CHAPTER 7

Breaking Down Barriers

Shaunagh Brown

RUGBY UNION PLAYER

*'It takes emotional bravery to be different
and stand your ground, but it's worth it.'*

When Shaunagh Brown remembers her second ever try scored
for England, a smile breaks out on her face. It was April 2022.
England were thirty-six points ahead of Wales in the Women's
Six Nations tournament, and a record 15,000-strong crowd had
descended on Gloucester's Kingsholm Stadium to cheer on the
Red Roses and watch them edge closer to Grand Slam victory.

*I'd been on the bench and I came on for the last fifteen minutes.
One player made a break. Everyone was running and the ball
got passed again and again. I was out on the wing. As a prop*

I should not have been anywhere near the wing, but when flanker Marlie Packer passed me the ball I had to embrace it. I caught it in loads of space, and when I looked around there were no defenders. I kept thinking, 'Oh shit.' I looked around again. There were no defenders in front of me so I just kept running and running. It's the fastest I'd ever run in an England shirt. When I slammed the ball down I thought, 'Wow, I've just scored a running try.' I had to hope for the best and it paid off. It felt so amazing.

Shaunagh's first try had only been scored two weeks earlier against Italy. And while the try itself hadn't been so dramatic, the scoreline was. England sent their rivals packing with a 74-0 win, but by that time no one was surprised. For the last three years Shaunagh had been part of a dominant England side that had fans like me hooked. Before her retirement in 2022 she had clocked up thirty caps for England. Not bad for someone who didn't play her first game of rugby until the age of twenty-five and went from rookie to international rugby star in just under two years.

And it's her total fearlessness both on and off the pitch that I'm struck by when we speak. When Shaunagh did finally bow out of the game at the end of 2022 aged thirty-two, England women's head coach Simon Middleton paid tribute to her positivity and dedication to being the best – a person who attacked every opportunity, he said. Now Shaunagh is a passionate advocate for the women's game, as well as a champion for inclusion and diversity. As a former gas engineer turned commercial diver, firefighter turned rugby player, she's also a woman who continues to turn female stereotypes on their head. Given that traditionally rugby has been an outlier sport for girls, I was interested to know whether the game piqued Shaunagh's interest from a young age.

Not at all. I didn't know anything about rugby until I was twenty-one. Where I grew up in south London there were no playing fields at school. It was also seen as a sport played in private schools and by middle-class white men. There was no reason for me to have come across it. There wasn't a white man in my house and no one was middle class. I grew up with my English mum, my brother who is ten years older than me and my sister who is sixteen years older. My dad, who is Jamaican, was around but he never lived with us.

I was also the only person in my family to pursue sports. We were an active family, but I think the only reason I was sporty and boisterous was because my brother and sister were so much older, so I grew up around my boy cousins. I wanted to play with them. I never thought of it as girl power. I just wanted to fight them, race them and be better than them. And I was lucky enough to have a family that let me do that.

I also think because of that I was never forced to do what was expected of me as a girl. People knew never to buy me a Barbie doll. My toy was an Action Man. And I didn't dress in pink because I didn't want to. At school there was one time I was upside down on the monkey bars wearing a skirt with my knickers on show and everyone laughed at me. I went home and said to Mum, 'I'm never wearing a dress again.' Fortunately, the school let me wear trousers and so I never felt inhibited being active. It makes me mad to this day that while schools want girls to pursue sports they insist on the uniform being a skirt with no option to wear trousers.

In fact, from the outset Shaunagh was an unconventional girl who would go down an unconventional route before she ever set foot on a rugby pitch, beginning her formal sporting career in shot-put and discus events. Yet her enthusiasm for all sports started at her primary school in Kennington in south-east London and continued throughout secondary, where she developed a talent for a wide variety of disciplines.

I enjoyed sport at primary school but I wasn't seeking it out. I just did it. If I wanted to play football I played with the boys and I'd play in a cage. But I'd also play on any apparatus or chalk squares on the floor. You could make a game out of anything. One of the first medals I won was when micro-scooters came out and I saved up all my birthday money and found a cheap £40 scooter. At school sports day that year they had the usual egg and spoon and three-legged events but they added an extra event which was a scooter race. It was once round the playground. I thought, 'Whoa!' I wasn't particularly fast at races, but I won it and it felt fantastic.

At secondary school we had trampolines and there was football, netball and basketball. One day I saw a red asterisk next to my name in the register and when I asked what that meant, the teacher said, 'It's so everyone knows that you're a bit special and you can do everything. We can put you in any group and you'll do well.' Until then I knew I was good at sport but only because I was happy doing it, but seeing it written down and having a teacher tell me that I was good was a real boost.

While Shaunagh says she was always supported by her teachers she also experienced what many girls who pursue sport go through, including me. As a hockey player I was often told by my peers that I was uncool or they called me a lesbian, which sadly was never said as a compliment. As a teenager I had to be strong not to let the name-calling get to me and fortunately I had the support and encouragement of my family. I wondered if Shaunagh experienced the same and how she dealt with it.

Because I did sport with the boys I got told all the time that I was bisexual or gay or I wanted to be trans or I was called a boy or a man all the time. Because of that I never felt my ability as a girl was celebrated. I was also physically well built and very strong. That made me even less cool. I always chose to play sports like football because I enjoyed them. And I also knew there were girls at school who secretly wanted to choose football but they didn't because it wasn't seen as the cool thing to do.

I remember asking my mum, 'Why are people calling me a boy? Why are they calling me gay?' I didn't even know what that was. My mum said they were just jealous and I needed to carry on doing what I loved. I was also fortunate that teachers stepped in and supported me if I was being picked on. They'd say to any bullies that I was just better at sport, so it helped that I had constant back-up from adults to keep going and to ignore it.

Yet what really changed Shaunagh's life was when teachers put her forward for a mini-marathon trial which led her to finding one of the only athletics clubs in south-east London she could go to that was affordable and accessible by public transport. There, she found like-minded athletes and felt at home. Up until that point, other than the sport she'd played at school, she'd never been welcomed as a girl in organized sport. Like me, she wanted to play football but hadn't been allowed to join a boys' team once she got to secondary age (at that time under FA rules, girls aged over eleven years old couldn't play in boys' teams), and no girls' teams existed in her area.

Transport was also a consideration. So many sporting stories start with mums, dads or a wider pool of relatives or family friends driving kids to practice and club matches. Shaunagh grew up in an inner city, reliant on public transport. For kids growing up in rural areas with an even less regular bus or train service, making a commitment to a sport they love can be tough. Certainly, I have my parents to thank for being a taxi service week in, week out. But for Shaunagh to have got there by herself takes real balls in my view.

My teachers put me forward for the trials to run 2.6 miles but I needed to go to an athletics track to do that. Mum suggested that while I was there I should enquire about joining. And that's how I started turning up on a Monday and Wednesday to the Blackheath Harriers (now the Blackheath and Bromley Harriers). The club was a satellite track of the main club in Bromley, and it was the only track I could get to on my own. Mum didn't drive, and the Bromley track would have been a 45-minute walk from the station, whereas this track was a ten-minute walk from the station so I could walk on my own.

At the club there were lots of runners, but after joining I quickly realized running wasn't for me. I wasn't good at it and I didn't enjoy it. I asked the coach, 'Is there anything else I can do?' She said, 'Yes, there are throwing events. But the coach for shot-put and discus is at the Bromley track. There's no one here to coach you.' Instead, she'd been reading a manual about how to teach shot-put and suggested that if I read it too I could teach myself and she would support me, and that's how I started.

As I improved, the coach did come over from the Bromley track to see me and he wanted to get me there, but in the end that only worked because someone volunteered to pick me up from the station every week. Someone making that commitment was so important. Now I coach girls in rugby on a Sunday and

I will offer to pick them up if they can't get there on public transport or if they can't afford the fare. I just want them there. Any girl who shows a remote interest I want to support to keep them playing.

That commitment from Shaunagh and the commitment of dedicated volunteers led to her competing at national championships in shot-put and discus as well as international junior and world youth events. Eventually she went on to represent England in the hammer throw at the 2014 Commonwealth Games in Glasgow. By that time, she'd left school, was in her early twenties and had trained as a British Gas engineer. Her sporting career would also not have been possible had the company not supported her too.

There were very few women doing my job at British Gas, and by that time I was … training in Loughborough a couple of times a week. I'd also moved out to Kent and so that was a long journey. I asked the company if I could drop down to three days a week, have some extra money to cover lost wages and use the company van to drive to training. I asked and they said yes.

The request had to go through a lot of bureaucracy, but they wanted to help me. Much later when I started playing rugby and I switched to a role in the fire service, it also agreed to help me out. I asked if I could change from being a front-line firefighter to doing a desk job to accommodate my rugby career.

Again, they said yes. When I asked them why they wanted to help me, one of my managers said, 'You asked, and you asked nicely and you didn't automatically expect it.' I think lots of people, especially women, are afraid to ask for help, but I was never afraid to. I was always up front about what I wanted. The worst someone can say is 'no'.

Yet throwing events aren't always an obvious choice for women, let alone black ethnic minority women. I know myself that being mixed-race Chinese I often felt out of place in hockey, which remains a predominantly white sport. I wondered whether Shaunagh ever felt like an outsider as a woman and as a mixed-race woman in particular.

When I was competing I was good and I was winning and so I was always celebrated. But I was the only mixed-race person doing throws. Black people tended to sprint and sometimes competed in long jump, but never throws.

In that respect I felt that I brought the team together because while I was competing in athletics I hung around with both my black friends who were runners and my throwing friends who were white. The two groups didn't really mix before I came along, whereas I wanted to talk to everyone. But it did make me question why all the sprinters are black. Is there an assumption that's what they'll be good at? However, that's not always the case and maybe people are stereotyped too early. Thankfully things are changing, though.

As for racism, I never experienced it directly in the UK, but I certainly did while travelling in athletics. As a thrower I went to Serbia, Russia and Bosnia – not very diverse places. People openly stopped black or mixed-race competitors like me in the street and asked if they could take a photograph. At first it seemed funny, but then I thought, 'No. Go away.'

So, how did an international thrower ever set foot on a pitch playing a sport she knew nothing about? Shaunagh's willingness to try anything is the answer. After she retired from athletics she even gave boxing a go. And while she describes herself as tough, she admits that once she'd taken a couple of hard blows to the head she decided boxing wasn't the sport for her. Rugby, however, satisfied all of Shaunagh's strengths. The first time she ever got to learn about the game was while training in athletics. At the track, she met male players who suggested she try it. But when she did eventually walk through the doors of her local club in Kent, I wondered whether she embraced the contact element of the game straight away.

It really suited me. Girls are constantly told that they need to be quiet and calm down. They're told they need to do what ladies do and ladies aren't tough. They're told to stop being boisterous, or they're told to stop being rough. But I was all of those things.

In rugby you're not only celebrated for being rough and tough and aggressive, but you're told to be rougher, tougher and more aggressive. Unlike boxing, the aim of the game is to get the ball past the line, not to knock someone out. So, the best part about rugby for me was the contact. Lots of girls feel they can't say it, but it was my greatest pleasure to run into someone with my hand shoved clean into their face and to push them over. And in rugby it's okay to like that. I'm not an aggressive person, but I am big and strong and there's no other legitimate outlet for it. I can't go around slamming doors or pushing people in the street, but on the rugby pitch I can use my speed, strength and power to my advantage.

When I found my local club which was Medway, I attended a first trial session. When I went back the second time the coach introduced me to the other girls. He said, 'This is Shaunagh. She's going to be very good.' I thought, 'How do you know?' But I guess he saw something in me. In that session we practised what's called pick and goes, where you pick the ball up from the floor and run until someone lands you on the floor. Because I was so strong, I ran with three girls hanging off me until a fourth eventually pulled me down. The physical side of rugby came easily to me, but what I found far harder was learning how to play the game, and learning to be in a team. Finding my place in a team yet keeping my own identity and knowing what I could offer took far more adjustment.

I know that in any team, having the confidence to be true to yourself can be hard, especially as a young player stepping into an established team culture.

Shaunagh admits that being an outsider in a local club was a tough transition to make. And while she loved playing and learning about the game of rugby, she found other aspects of being part of a team more challenging. How did she develop the confidence to be herself?

To be honest, I probably didn't fully develop real confidence until I was in my final year playing for England, but at Medway I did start that journey.

It was a great club to begin my training at and I enjoyed playing. However, what was tough was that I was an outsider who rocked up and the coach thought I was fantastic. At moments he was changing the game plan to give me the ball. Others weren't being given that opportunity. It didn't affect my game because I always wanted to play at my best, but there were other aspects where my difference stood out. At heart, I was a south London girl. I spoke differently. The music I listened to was different. My music was Jamaican bashment, soca, Afrobeat and reggae. I don't drink much alcohol and in all rugby teams – male and female – there's often a drinking culture. Sometimes I did find it emotionally draining to say I didn't want to take part in drinking games and I was often accused of being boring. I think sometimes groups feel threatened by someone who is different. I wasn't a bad thing, I was just a different thing. In the end I accepted that I was different and carried on turning up for the sport which I loved.

Yet it was that focused attitude that most impressed the England head coach Simon Middleton when Shaunagh attended her first England camp. By then she'd watched the Red Roses play at the Twickenham Stoop and at that moment set her sights on an international career. However, she knew that if she wanted to play for her national side she would have to join a Premiership team, which Medway wasn't. To realize that ambition she made the move to Harlequins whose training ground was in Guildford. Even though Shaunagh was still living in Kent, it was her nearest top-flight club despite being more than an hour from home.

Being at the Stoop that day was the first time I decided I was going to play rugby for England. It was 2016 and Mum and I had gone to see a Six Nations game. I turned to her and said, 'I'm going to play for England one day.' She said, 'Okay.' She didn't doubt me. Because I'd said it out loud I knew I had to make it happen and I put a lot of pressure on myself to achieve it.

After I started playing for Harlequins, that's when I got picked for the England camp for the first time. Afterwards, Simon Middleton sat me down and asked me how I'd found it. I said, 'I'm not here to make friends. I'm here to play rugby.' Often people do say they're there to make friends, whereas I thought of making friends as a lovely addition, but I didn't feel I had to get on swimmingly with everyone. I needed to have a civilized relationship with my teammates, but I didn't feel I had to please everyone or that we all had to be the same. Apparently he loved that because women never say it.

However, what I did learn was that if I got to know people off the pitch it often made me want to play more for them on the pitch. If I knew that a teammate had been working in the gym for a month to improve her strength to win more tackles and she went out and won more, I'd understand how much that tackle meant to her. That, to me, was what made a team.

Shaunagh played in the prop position for England, a position she started in when she first began playing for Medway. I was interested in how she gravitated to prop and, being such an independent character, how she handled some of the more prescriptive elements of the game.

I wasn't actually the right size or height for a prop, but I was big and strong and Medway needed a prop. Being a prop is all about good positioning. In the scrum you need a flat back and strong legs. When I went to Harlequins the coach Karen Findlay felt I was wasted in that position and put me in the back row, so that's where I started my professional career. But when I began to play for England, full-time contracts had just been introduced. It was felt I wasn't fit enough or couldn't run fast enough to play back row, and England needed a prop. They offered to fully train me if I took a contract, so I agreed.

That said, I was definitely a more creative player. Usually in rugby everyone should know what they are doing for the whole eighty minutes of the game. There's not a lot of free thinking in some teams and that didn't always work for me. Sometimes if a coach did change the team's way of thinking that felt refreshing and I loved coaches who said, 'Just play. Just go where you are needed on the pitch.' Other players needed the reassurance of knowing where they needed to be at any given moment, but I was always a more curious person in the beginning. At training camp I always sat at the front with my notebook and pen and I asked lots of questions, often all the questions others were afraid to ask. Sometimes if I suggested a new way to play I was shot down, but it never stopped me from asking and making myself vulnerable in those early days.

Through being true to myself my confidence grew. Even in small things. There would have been a time when I wouldn't have added my music to the changing-room playlist because no one else listened to my music and it would get shouted down. But over time I was defending my choice: this is my track. I put it on. It takes emotional bravery to be different and stand your ground, but it's worth it.

But while rugby embraced Shaunagh and her unique style, it's taken far longer for the wider world to embrace the women's game. Certainly, the history of women's rugby remains largely untold, simply because teams or matches were never documented. During the Victorian era, women playing was seen as socially unacceptable and many were forced to play in secret. Organized women's rugby league teams started appearing in the north of England in the early 1950s, the league game being notably different for having thirteen players instead of union's fifteen as well as a different points system and tackling rules which evolved over time.

Even in 2014 when the Red Roses won the World Cup against Canada – their first World Cup win in twenty years – women's rugby was hardly the buzzword on everyone's lips. Yet fast-forward to today, and it's a different story. Now players like Emily Scarratt, former Red Roses captain Sarah Hunter, Tamara Taylor, Rochelle Clark and Shaunagh among others are household names to followers. In almost a decade, the profile and popularity of the women's game has surged and turned it into one of the fastest growing team sports in the world. Around 2.7 million women and girls now play at school, in the professional leagues and for their countries. In England, the Rugby Football Union (RFU) has ambitious targets to grow the number of women playing at the grassroots level from its current 40,000 to 100,000 by 2027. At the elite level, women playing both rugby sevens and fifteens are enjoying the benefits of professional contracts, the latter only being introduced in 2019. But if women's rugby is to grow, how does it attract a more diverse talent pool – people like Shaunagh – who don't know about the game?

The problem is before you even get to rugby. Rugby development officers visit the same schools. For example, in the men's game all the Premiership teams have academies and they'll advertise the fact that ten boys have been promoted from the academy into the first team. But sometimes eight out of those ten boys will likely have come from the same school.

If you are going to the same places you are going to get the same people. Rugby needs to start looking for talent in different places, especially if they want to grow the women's game. They need to look at rugby clubs and where they are – can you get there by public transport? If someone wants to step up to the next stage, the nearest club might be miles away. They need to ask some questions. How long is the walk? Is the walk floodlit? If a person is religious is there somewhere in the club they can pray? Are the changing rooms clean? Are there soft drinks available? Is there a space where someone can breastfeed their child? In other words, is this a space that welcomes a different kind of person? Outside of play these are the things that are important. So many clubs put up a sign that says 'We Welcome All' and they think that's job done, but it isn't.

As for women's rugby, Shaunagh is still one of only a handful of players from a black ethnic minority background. Despite the RFU's commitment to diversity, the game remains predominantly white although the landscape does appear to be shifting. In Scotland, Panashe Muzambe became the first woman of colour to be capped in 2019. And in the 2021 World Cup, Shaunagh was one of four black ethnic minority members of a thirty-two-strong England team, the highest number the team has had since Shaunagh joined.

When it comes to the game's governance, former England international Maggie Alphonsi remains the only person of colour to sit on the RFU's council as a permanent member, although women have been a part of it since 2013. (In 2021, the RFU seconded three black ethnic minority members to the committee for a fixed period until 2023 including female player Garnet Mackinder.) Until 2021, the RFU board of directors was exclusively white until it appointed British black entrepreneur Tom Ilube as RFU chairman. Does Shaunagh believe there is a meaningful commitment to change?

Rugby is 200 years old and there are people coming into the game who are thinking differently. It will take a while for the wheels to turn, but there are initiatives around that do tackle structure and change. I believe there is an appetite for change but that has only come about in the last three years. Initially I was part of a panel called Rugby Against Racism, but that turned out to be a non-entity for me. It came after the Black Lives Matter protests. We took the knee for a season and then forgot about it. It was nothing more than a statement.

However, there is an RFU initiative called Rugby United which specifically targets black and South Asian people. It engages schools and community clubs and tries to break down barriers that exist to bringing more players from those areas into the game. And now, when I look at women's rugby there are some good things happening. A couple of years ago, a graffiti mural was painted at Twickenham featuring Emily Scarratt,

Zoe Harrison and me. Sarah Hunter has her own mural at her home club in Newcastle. Emily also has a mural at Leicester. As I didn't have a home club, I have a mural on the Oval in Kennington near where I grew up.

By commissioning these, immediately you are telling a different person they can play rugby. A marketing company was also hired to help us spread the word. As much as I've featured in the Guardian *or the* Telegraph *or even on Radio 5 Live, this is not what I read or listened to growing up. But now I've spoken on Capital XTRA radio, Rinse FM and I've been in* The Voice *newspaper. I knew about these growing up. If you want a different audience, you need to promote players to a different audience.*

And it's not just increasing diversity that rugby's governing body has in its in tray. Growing concern over safety has also sparked debate over whether contact sports such as rugby should be played at school at all.

For professionals, high-profile campaigns around the increased risk of motor neurone disease spearheaded by former players such as rugby league superstar Rob Burrow have prompted calls to better protect competitors. Meanwhile, research suggests that female players could be twice as likely as men to develop sports-related dementia due to concussion. While studies are ongoing, hormonal differences between the sexes may be one explanation. Higher concussion rates may also be because women's neck muscles are weaker than men's, giving them less control during contact. As a player who relished the contact element of the sport, I was interested to hear Shaunagh's thoughts on whether safety concerns might put off girls, or stop the sport being made available to more children?

In schools, teachers are nervous of both boys and girls doing full contact sports. Rugby is perceived as aggressive and people do think it's a given that you are going to get hurt, which is not the case.

When I think about my own experience, I didn't start playing until I was twenty-five so I don't always think contact is the most important element of the sport initially. When I coach now, I get kids passing and throwing rugby balls first and then if they want to build to contact that can come later or they can go to their local club.

And there are also safe, sterile ways of practising contact. Teachers can use pads and tackle bags. Even as adults we had a crash mat to fall on to so we weren't hitting the floor every time. There are ways of controlling the contact very easily and I think for young people that's the best way to introduce them to the game.

Once she began playing professionally, did Shaunagh have any reservations about safety and does she think enough is being done to protect players?

The medical staff I worked with at the elite level looked after us almost better than we looked after ourselves. They were constantly advising us whether we should train or play so I always felt very safe in that respect. Sometimes a doctor would tell me, 'you are physically able to play if you want to, but at the moment I wouldn't advise it'. Then, it would be up to me and I generally followed the advice. Sometimes I was stubborn around concussion. If I felt fine [after a concussion] and I'd been able to recite the months of the year backwards then I wanted to play, but mostly I was adult about it.

However, when it comes to safety I believe it has to run from the medical team through to every member of staff including coaches. Sometimes I did have reservations about how I was being told to tackle, for example if I was asked to hit a rolling maul (a group of players who collectively move forward to protect the ball carrier) head on. I didn't always feel comfortable airing those reservations, so the way I dealt with it was to hit the maul in a way that was comfortable for me, where I knew I wasn't going to get a foot in my head. So, there does need to be standards around safety that everyone follows and that's probably where I see that improvements can be made.

Also, in Shaunagh's view, meaningful improvement must be made when it comes to women achieving equality in the game. Headlines, particularly around equal pay, look good, she says, but the small print still doesn't always reflect the reality.

It's nice that women are being celebrated in the game. And it's nice that it's not just us putting ourselves out there, but that some governing bodies are doing it and they want to keep pushing. I benefited from being on a professional contract, and by women being given that option we are raising the bar. Now people have seen the fruits of our labours on the pitch. But the reality is that while all UK nations now have professional contracts, some female players may only be paid £8,000 a year, which means they still have to work. When you look at the men's game, some professional contracts start at around £30,000. So, there's work to be done there.

As for raising the bar, the England women's team has more than hit that mark. Not only is the women's Six Nations competition thriving, but the 2022 World Cup final between England and New Zealand attracted 2.65 million TV viewers in the UK alone, the largest single audience for a women's Rugby World Cup final ever. I loved every moment of that tournament and was gutted to watch England being beaten by just three points in a final that ended a winning run of thirty matches for the team. Sport can be cruel but, for me, the tense drama throughout was a signifier that women's rugby has arrived and its passionate rivalries and inspirational talent are now being given the platform they deserve.

As a final thought, though, I wanted to know how the team, and Shaunagh, coped as the team's winning streak came to a close.

If we'd have won that game it would have gone down as one of the greatest games in women's history. But a loss is a loss. It was gutting, but afterwards we all came together. We sang on the bus all the way home. Adele featured quite a bit on our playlist because everyone knew the words and we could all join in. We sing after any match – whether we win or lose. Sometimes we sing happy songs, sometimes sad songs, but whatever the score we sing. For all the differences that individuals in a team bring, we are in it together. We worked hard together, we played together and we lost together.

CHAPTER 8

For the Love of Sport

Sheila Parker MBE

FOOTBALLER AND FIRST ENGLAND CAPTAIN

'If the ban had been lifted earlier, women would have got to where we are now much quicker. We loved the game and all we wanted to do was play.'

It was during half-time at England's friendly against the USA at Wembley in October 2022 when Sheila Parker went out on to the pitch with other surviving members of the first ever Lionesses team. In front of a crowd of 78,000 she stood behind the England flag alongside players from the current Euro-winning Lioness squad including captain Leah Williamson and forward Beth Mead. That day, Sheila and her former teammates were presented with their first ever official England caps despite having stormed to victory fifty years earlier. In that year, 1972, the Lionesses played and won their debut international against Scotland on a freezing, muddy pitch in the Scottish borders. That it has taken so long for the team to be recognized is a source of much frustration, not only for Sheila but for so many women who fought to play football. Yet for the 75-year-old, that reception is also the source of so much pride.

Going on to that pitch, I've never seen anything like it. It was overwhelming. There were so many women, and quite a lot of men too, there to watch the women's game. It was completely the opposite of my day. I led the squad out in my wheelchair with my friend Vanessa pushing me. She was in tears, but I couldn't cry. I was too excited. When an announcement boomed over the tannoy, the whole stadium stood up and cheered. To be honest, I felt really embarrassed by all the attention.

Later, after we'd been presented with our caps, Leah Williamson asked to have her photo taken with me. She wanted to stand with the Lionesses' original captain. She told me that without the 1972 squad the 2022 team would not be there. She told me that we were the pioneers. Although it was lovely to hear Leah say that, I'd never thought of myself as being part of the journey to where women's football is now. Now it makes me so proud to know that I was a member of a team that made it all possible.

Women are coming into sport and into the world in a way that they have never done before, and it's fantastic that young girls playing the game now might think, 'I could play for England one day.'

That Sheila is so humble about her contribution to women's football was very moving to hear. Yet to understand why it's unbelievable for her to see how far the women's game has come, I wanted to go back in time to appreciate what Sheila and her teammates had to endure to put women's football on the map. Having myself been banned from the local boys' team, the Wirral Panthers, aged nine, I understand some of the prejudices that existed around girls playing, but I was fortunate enough to have the choice of later joining the women's team at Tranmere Rovers, based in Birkenhead. When Sheila first started playing in the 1950s, not only were there few women's teams in existence, but they had all been banned from playing on the Football Association's affiliated grounds – a ban that had been in place since 1921, the reasons for which ranged from an FA belief that football was unsuitable for women to an underlying fear that the rising popularity of the women's game and the money raised through ticket sales were beyond FA control. For Sheila, it was a ruling she believes held back progress of the women's game for decades.

When the Lionesses won 2-1 in the Euro final against Germany in July 2022, I watched it at home and I nearly fell off the couch when Chloe Kelly scored that winning goal. The women played brilliantly. I did think it was going to go to penalties but I was

confident that if it did, Mary Earps would keep any goals out.
She had been brilliant all tournament. And if Leah Williamson
was nervous about being captain it didn't show.

But I did have to pinch myself. I did think about what it
would have felt like had it been me, or what it would have felt
like to play in front of that crowd, knowing all these people
were watching. If the ban had been lifted earlier, women would
have got to where we are now much, much quicker. We loved
the game and all we wanted to do was play.

In fact, Sheila wanted to play so badly that as a young girl
growing up in the small town of Chorley in Lancashire she
begged, borrowed and stole a game wherever she could. What
was it about football that drew her in, I wondered?

I was one of three children, and I was the only one who played.
My brother and sister didn't, and my parents weren't watchers
of the sport. My dad's eyesight was very poor so he wouldn't
have been able to enjoy it, and my mum just wasn't into it. None
of my family were football-minded, but there was something in
my genes saying, 'You have to play football.' It was fate, I think.

As a girl, I certainly couldn't play football at school. Girls
were offered netball or hockey, so as a young girl I used to
go down to Chorley recreation ground. The lads used to play
down there. Those would have been lads I went to school
with or friends from the street. I remember watching from the
sidelines and I asked, 'Can I play?' They said, 'No, girls don't

play football!' But something in me continued to turn up to watch, and when I started kicking a ball around on my own, the lads noticed I was quite good so they asked me to join in. Then they said, 'My God. I'm glad she's playing with us.' Every time I turned up I wondered if they'd let me play with them again, but they did and that gave me a really good feeling.

Playing with boys can be a mixed experience. When I started playing in our back garden with my brother and his mates, I did learn a lot of technique from them. I'd copy their moves and add my own flair. But I also never wanted to be treated differently. I didn't want them to think they had to compensate for the fact that I was a girl. What was the play like in Sheila's day?

At first some of the boys were afraid to tackle me and I said, 'Just play football! If I go down I go down.' Falling or getting muddy didn't bother me at all. And I learned from them too. I tried to pick up some of the passes and I got good at free kicks and defending and also slide tackling. I loved slide tackling.

I also used to go to watch the men play at my local club, Chorley FC. When I was young I'd have to save up my pocket money to go and watch. I was lucky in that no one in my family ever told me I wasn't to go or it was wrong for me to go. My parents said that if I enjoyed it then I should, but I don't remember women in the stands. Women were at home with families, not shouting on the terraces.

When Sheila was thirteen, she joined Dick, Kerr Ladies, one of a number of women's teams in the area that that had grown from women being employed in factory work. While by no means the first ladies' team in the North West, Dick, Kerr's had a long heritage born from the First World War when women were recruited into munitions factories. The Preston-based company Dick, Kerr & Co started out manufacturing locomotives and rolling stock but moved to producing shells during the war. Its women's football team developed out of lunchtime kickabouts to where games were played in aid of charity. And it produced players like the famous Lily Parr, the best ever women's goalscorer who scored 900 goals during her thirty-year career.

By the end of the Great War, women's football had reached a peak. Dick, Kerr's were attracting almost 50,000 spectators to matches. One game against St Helens Ladies on Boxing Day 1920 attracted a crowd of 53,000 at Goodison Park with thousands locked outside the ground. However, in 1921 when there were around 150 women's football clubs, the Football Association decided football was 'quite unsuitable for women' and their 'delicate frames' and refused them use of its pitches for matches. By the time Sheila began playing around 1960, the ban was still firmly in place, but against the odds factory teams kept playing with many of them, including Dick, Kerr's, still raising money for charity.

The atmosphere in the team was great – there was lots of camaraderie. I remember all the women there loved playing the game and they couldn't understand why men didn't want them to play.

For that reason we all wanted to stick together. I would have been one of the youngest and I would have played with women of all ages. In those days women didn't have much freedom of speech so we did things in other ways. Football was one of the few ways we could express ourselves.

But at Dick, Kerr's I would have had to save up and buy my own kit. All we got given was a bucket, cold water, sponge and a freeze spray for injury. I'd be out there in my shin pads and the ball was a heavy leather-stitched ball. These days, no one would be allowed to play on the pitches we played on. Because we couldn't play on FA grounds we played on rugby pitches or scrubland or recreational grounds and school fields. It was rough and ready, and we'd be playing in frost, ice, snow and rain. If you went down on the pitch then you could break bones, and sometimes the mud would be inches thick, and you'd go home covered in mud and have to wash your own kit. When I walked around the dressing rooms at Wembley with Jill Scott and Leah Williamson, it was like Buckingham Palace for football. I couldn't believe it.

Having followed closely the fortunes of today's Lionesses, I wondered whether Sheila also felt the women's game itself had changed.

The play was definitely different in my day. We did a lot more passing of the ball. These days there's more kicking the ball up the pitch which we didn't do. The game seems far more tactical now. Our game was simple: pass the ball to each other up the field and get it into the back of the net.

When we talked about the game with today's Lionesses at Wembley, I think they were a bit shocked. We didn't have anything that clubs have today. We didn't have coaches working with individual players. We didn't have video analysis. We just went on to the pitch and kicked the ball around. The team managers and the coaches were from the community and usually they were a husband or a brother or a relative of one of the ladies who played. Everything was a community affair. There wasn't anything like a sport psychologist. The coaches simply said, 'Go out, enjoy the game and do your best to win.'

What's harder for me to imagine is that women didn't even have a league to play in until after 1969. Although history suggests that women playing football is not a new thing – it was claimed that in the sixteenth century, Mary Queen of Scots owned the oldest football in existence – women trying to organize themselves into a league didn't happen until 1881. One of the first teams, Mrs Graham's XI, had its debut match at Edinburgh's Easter Road stadium, but further games were called off due to violent pitch invasions from those who believed only men should play. The objections were varied from football being considered too damaging to women's health to it being unbecoming for a woman wearing a dress to play. There was also a fear that women might charge for tickets and make money from games – all of which smacked of professionalism. Eventually early attempts at establishing a league in the 1880s were abandoned, not to be resurrected until almost 100 years later.

By then the England men's team had clinched World Cup victory against Germany at Wembley in 1966. In response, the Women's Football Association (WFA) was formed, initially with forty-four member clubs and headed by volunteer women and men desperate to see the women's game flourish and the ban lifted. In the North West, a women's league was also established initially comprising of eight teams. I was interested in Sheila's recollections of that time and how the 1966 victory gave momentum to the women's fight.

We didn't have footballing heroines because we didn't see them on TV. We only knew the women we played with. But I do remember watching men's football on television. I loved to watch Bobby Charlton. He was a great all-rounder. He could play in any position, and I was the same. He always seemed to be in possession of the ball but he was always up front scoring goals too. Whenever I watched the men's game, I always imagined myself being on TV and playing football but it was a fantasy. At that time, we knew it was never going to be a reality. It was too far out of reach.

I do recall the 1966 World Cup. I was at home. It was very exciting and there was definitely a feeling among us that we

should also have that chance, but there was no outlet for it.
We didn't even have a league in 1966, so as much as women
wanted something, we couldn't do much to drive it forward.

The Women's FA, however, did drive that desire forward. Later
it would have an office based in Manchester, but initially it was
a loose affiliation. It advertised for women players on the back
of match flyers and also fundraised continually to progress
the women's game. By that time, Dick, Kerr's had folded as a
team, apparently due to dwindling numbers, and Sheila had
started playing for Fodens Ladies FC, the works team for Edwin
Foden, Sons & Co, a transport manufacturing company based
in nearby Sandbach. There, Sheila played with outstanding
women such as the late Sylvia Gore and Jeannie Allott. Funnily
enough, I came across Sylvia when I began training at the Centre
of Excellence for football in Merseyside in the 1990s where
Sylvia was one of the directors. By then she was well into her
fifties and I do recall being scared of her. She was caring, but
tough. You knew where you stood with Sylvia.

Sylvia was a really good player. She definitely had something
special. But all of the women were committed to the game.
After I left school I began working for Leyland Motors as a
receptionist. I'd do a day's work then I'd do some training after
work on most nights. I'd train with Fodens maybe two or three
times a week and then I'd run on my own on other evenings.
And once the league started we weren't just trying to get a game

with the local Scout groups or other lads' or works' teams, we started travelling to matches.

We'd go to Cumbria or Manchester or elsewhere and that's when the game really started growing, and the interest in women joining a team grew too. For those of us who were already playing we thought it was great. Travelling around broadened our horizons.

And with our own league we had a purpose. It made us very independent. We'd share a car to go to the matches and we'd chip in to buy petrol and pay for our kits. Everything was pay to play, and we'd also have to chip in for a game and for referees' fees and pitch fees. We had to do a lot of fundraising – it might have been a sponsored walk or a bike ride or tombolas or raffles just to get the money together to play. We were determined.

With mounting pressure on the FA to lift the ban on women playing at their football grounds, the ruling was eventually abandoned in 1971, although the FA didn't issue an official apology until 1983. By then Sheila was married and had a young son, Darren. It was hard enough to be a woman footballer in those days, so I was interested to hear whether as a footballing mother, she was judged.

When I had my son I didn't play for around nine months. That was my maternity break, but I thought about football a lot. Not only had it kept me fit, but I missed being with all the women

I played with. We did keep in touch and so I always had it in my mind that I was going to go back.

When I did start playing again I used to take my son Darren with me. He'd sit in his buggy on the side of the pitch and friends would look after him while I played. At Fodens there may have been some other young mothers playing but it was very rare. I do remember one or two people, including women themselves, telling me that I should have been at home changing nappies and looking after the baby. I ignored it. I always thought those people didn't know me or understand what I was doing. I thought, 'Think what you like. This is what I'm going to do.' That was my character.

With the ban lifted, women were free to play on FA grounds, but very little else changed overnight. For many years to come, few resources were given to women's league teams. Playing at previously off-limits grounds also had its obstacles, Sheila explains.

Even at that time we weren't playing on brilliant pitches. We used to play at places like Rossendale which was on a hill and if the ball ran down the hill someone would have to run to get it. You'd be waiting half an hour for them to bring it back.

Half the time we had no access to the changing rooms, either. The changing rooms were there, but if we got to use them it was only because the attendant remembered to open them for the women. The men played in the morning and we played in the afternoon. Either the changing rooms were shut by then or if we did have access to them then all the hot water would have been used. We'd get changed in the backs of cars or we'd go home covered in muck.

Yet, the amazing thing for me is that it didn't once stop women from turning up to play the game they loved. That said, Sheila's dreams were yet to be realized. In 1972 she went on to be chosen by England women's manager Eric Worthington alongside Sylvia Gore and Jeannie Allott to play in the first ever England squad in the first ever international game. On 18 November 1972, England would play against Scotland at Ravenscraig Stadium in Greenock. But Sheila wasn't only picked as an outstanding player, she was asked to captain the team. What marked her out was not simply her all-round playing style but also her leadership qualities.

In terms of my playing style, it's been said by others that no one knew from one game to the next what style I was going to play. Maybe I took my style from Bobby Charlton – a good all-rounder. I dotted about everywhere on the pitch and I was fast too, so I was hard to mark because of that. I found it easy to read the game from a variety of positions.

I don't remember being picked at all, but I wouldn't have gone for trials. Trials for women came later. I think in those early days word got around who the good players were and so I think I may have been picked after Eric came to see me play at Fodens through word of mouth. I don't know the specific reason why he picked me, but maybe he saw the range of football I played.

What I do remember is that Eric understood how women played football and most importantly he understood that we wanted to play. But his message was always that we should enjoy the game. He said if we were doing a sport we loved then winning would naturally come from that. In that sense, it was relaxed. Anything too strict and I think I would have walked away.

As for my leadership qualities, I didn't see that in myself at all. And maybe that helped. I didn't ever think that being a captain was about me. I didn't ever want to be bigger than the team. There were probably a few characters with bigger egos but I suspect I ignored that. I didn't have much time for it. I just loved the sport and I had that passion. My team came first – some said before anything else, including my family. I was dedicated. As a captain I'd say I was firm but fair. As far as I was concerned we had a job to do on the pitch and we needed to get that job done well.

But when I was chosen I was so excited and very thankful I'd been picked to play for the country. I always hoped I was good enough to play for England, but being picked was out of this world. I think one of the first people I told was my brother, Raymond. He was over the moon for me.

As well as being picked as captain, Sheila also became the first mother to have ever led a national women's football team. Even today, women fear pregnancy will derail their athletic careers and I was no different at the peak of my hockey career. I can only salute Sheila for leading her team out that day.

I was twenty-four years old at the time. My son was thirteen months old and he did come in the pushchair with his father. I vaguely remember travelling there on a coach. We never went anywhere on a coach and it was a long way to Greenock. And when we got there, the crowd felt really big but nothing compared to today's crowds. There were probably around 150 people watching.

The FA had advertised it around other women's clubs and some fundraised or chipped in together to get a minibus to come and watch the game. The team stayed in a hotel and I've read since that we had to wear a skirt for the whole time we were in the hotel. I don't recall that but I imagine none of us would have been too happy.

It was November and bitterly cold that day. Nowadays you wouldn't play on that pitch. It was icy and there was snow falling in the second half. At times we were skating around the pitch and probably not tackling as hard because if we'd have gone down we would have been badly injured.

We all knew Scotland were a tough team, but I couldn't have been prouder or more excited to lead the team out on to the pitch. Scotland led at half-time, but in the second half something just clicked and we were able to fight back and win 3-2. There were goals from Sylvia Gore, Lynda Hale and Jeannie Allott.

I don't remember being on the coach home, but I think we would have sung all the way – we often did. Or we'd go out for a meal to celebrate, or get takeaway fish and chips. To win it, it was marvellous and it really felt like the beginning of something.

Sadly however, what Sheila and the team were denied was their first official international cap. While the FA had lifted the pitch ban it still did not recognize the England women's team as a national team. I'll never forget receiving my first official hockey cap after a friendly against Argentina – it's up there with one of my proudest moments and I can only imagine how that lack of recognition must have stung Sheila and her teammates. In the end, the team did receive caps only because one very special member of the Women's FA stepped in to support the women, Sheila explains.

I could never understand why the FA refused to give us an official cap. We were all at the match. We all played that match, so it was right that we should have got an official cap, but none had been made. Instead, there was a woman called Flo Bilton who was one of the founding members and an officer of the WFA. She did lots of the administration behind the scenes and she looked after us. Flo was a lovely woman. Everything she did was voluntary. She was so committed to progressing women's football and we had a lot to thank her for.

In the run-up to that game, she made caps for all the women. They were hand-stitched by her and she made caps for three of our international games in the end. They were based on the men's caps and she copied the design. The cap was navy blue with an England crest sewn into the front and 'Scotland 1972' stitched into it. But Flo was getting on in age and couldn't keep making the caps, so when she stopped sewing them we started to receive shields.

Sheila went on to play under four England managers: Eric Worthington, John Adams, Tommy Tranter and Martin Reagan. By 1973, England remained unbeaten in all five matches that Sheila captained. In 1974, Sheila also became part of the women's FA Cup-winning side. The cup had been established in 1970, also organized by the Women's Football Association, and Sheila won with Fodens who clinched a 2-1 win over Southampton, at the time seen as a formidable team. In 1975 she moved to Preston North End Ladies FC and proved herself as a prolific goalscorer, propelling the team into Division One status.

In 1975, after I joined Preston North End Ladies, I scored a lot of goals for the team – fifty-one goals in fourteen games. We had some really good players and a fantastic goalkeeper like today's Mary Earps who didn't let any ball in.

As a team we had ambitions and we wanted to win things so we trained very hard too. I was playing every weekend, usually on a Sunday, and maybe training two or three times a week for a couple of hours. We had a reputation of being a good side with an attacking style and a difficult side to beat.

In total, Sheila also played thirty-three times for her country and was there when the England women's team spread their wings and travelled to places like Italy and Japan. At home and abroad, Sheila became recognizable for her trademark baseball cap covered in badges which she wore everywhere, as well as her reputation to lead a winning side.

The Japan tour was in 1981 and it was also to broaden our horizons. We played friendlies over there against Denmark, Italy and Japan. When it was announced, I thought brilliant! It was such an honour. I'd never been on a plane before let alone a long-haul flight. We went to Tokyo, and it was so different from England with its neon signs and different foods and customs. The games were played at Kobe Stadium. I never went anywhere without my baseball cap. It was covered in badges because I collected badges: some were football badges and others were from holidays and others I was given in Japan. I was badge mad. The Japanese loved that cap and I remember giving some of my badges to the children there who had turned up to the stadium.

In 1984, the year after Sheila retired from the England squad, the WFA became affiliated to the FA as a 'County Association', but it would be another ten years before the FA founded the Women's Football Committee to run women's football in England. That same year England lost to Sweden in the first UEFA competition for national women's teams –

the predecessor to the Women's Euros we enjoy today. The affiliation also led to more centralized support with twenty centres of excellence opened in the late 1990s, which I benefited from attending in Merseyside. But Sheila's retirement from the England squad didn't signal the end of her footballing career. In fact she would go on to be involved in the sport for another ten years, finally finishing her footballing days at Clitheroe Ladies FC.

When I retired completely from the England squad in 1983, I knew I couldn't carry on physically, but to leave it behind was very sad. But I still kept playing. I then became a player-manager of Chorley Ladies FC, because by then my local club, whom I'd always watched, had a women's team. I was well known locally too. We were in Division Two, but I was coming in with an England pedigree so I think the women respected me as a manager. I was always someone who wanted good feedback and gave good feedback. I encouraged an open conversation so that we were always improving. The team did quite well, but often I'd have to change tactics because the other teams got to know my style.

As for support, we might have had around twenty spectators for a game.

By the time I retired fully I was forty-six and I was refereeing by then. After, I had to be happy with watching football on television, but of course the women's game was not shown for many years. But whenever I could I followed the progress of the Lionesses. Their achievements have been amazing but I do feel very sad that the support didn't happen fifty years ago.

It is amazing also to think that there was no dedicated museum exhibition to record the largely untold history of women's football until very recently. Although many female players have been inaugurated into the Football Hall of Fame – Sheila was inducted in 2013 – it wasn't until 2017 that the museum based in Manchester started exploring and cataloguing its women's football collection for the first time.

My original cap made by Flo Bilton is now in the Football Hall of Fame along with my original England shirt and my shield. I know they are safe there and I also want others to see what the women's game was like so many years ago. When I was inaugurated, there was a speech about my career and I was presented with a trophy. It really was magic. Women's football at that time was all about women coming together as a community and supporting one another and it's an important story.

Now Sheila has finally been recognized with an official England cap, she says she will also donate that to the collection in the future. She was also awarded an MBE in 2021, a year before the Lionesses' historic Euro win. In response, the Lionesses tweeted their congratulations and posted a picture of the young Sheila on Instagram – a truly twenty-first-century way of honouring a footballing heroine. At her local ground, Chorley FC, Sheila also unveiled a plaque in 2022 to recognize her achievements not far from the stand she first sat in all those years ago. What does Sheila think, now that her and other women's stories are finally being told?

I didn't expect anything like this happening. I'm proud, but I'm also surprised. All I ever did was play for the love of the sport. There's so much money in the game now, but at the end of the day it's a sport and women should go out there and just enjoy it. Get involved. You will be accepted but if you have the need to play like I did, just get involved.

CHAPTER 9

Trust and Responsibility

Kate Richardson-Walsh OBE

HOCKEY PLAYER AND
FORMER ENGLAND WOMEN'S CAPTAIN

*'Winning is in moments when team cultures are
made and broken – the special times that no
one ever sees and no one ever talks about.'*

In training, we called it shovelling on the shit. It was that end-of-week feeling when our bodies ached with tiredness. Under floodlights, we could see the outline of our breath against the biting cold.

A pass would be made. A lazy, crap pass. Thirty seconds later another player would do the same. Suddenly, a shout pierced the air. 'STOP! EVERYONE IN!' It was the voice of Kate Richardson-Walsh, our captain. We'd lug ourselves towards her and hunker down in a circle.

'This is fucking shit,' she'd say. 'What are we training for? What are our team values? We're not here for nothing. Let's make this session count.' In a heartbeat, it was as if a reset button had been pressed – we shook off our 'that will do' attitude and our game revitalized.

Kate always commanded respect. She's a straight-talking northerner. Many of the younger team members, like me, were scared of her but that only made us keen to work hard for her. She had this innate knack of encouraging you or bollocking you at a time and a place that felt spot on.

Yet off the pitch, the Kate I got to know as a part of the women's GB team was different. She questioned herself. She owned failure even when it wasn't hers to own. Given those two sides to her character, I was fascinated to understand more about her leadership journey, especially now she's an ambassador for sport, promoting diversity, inclusion and female leadership.

When Kate and I first met, we didn't know we would ever play hockey together, let alone go on to win gold at the 2016 Rio Olympics. It was 2002 and I was a naive fourteen-year-old. That same year, she'd been crowned England women's captain – a role she held for thirteen years – and she'd been brought in as guest coach to our training session. An England women's international? It hadn't occurred to me that I could be that, but a switch got flicked. Kate wasn't aloof or untouchable. She was real and passionate. For the first time, I thought, 'Maybe one day I could play for Team GB too.'

To me, Kate appeared a natural leader. So what did it feel like to be picked as GB captain at the age of twenty-three? At the time, Kate explains, she was poised to compete in the Champions Trophy in Sydney. The women's hockey team had recently hired a new coach, the Australian Tricia Heberle, who had brought a fresh way of working to the team.

Tricia was the best communicator I'd had as a coach. She was really in tune with players. She'd hand-write cards to us after tournaments. They weren't about you as a hockey player. They were about you as a person and your development, and because of that players opened up.

As a team we voted in our captain, but so far Tricia had run a co-captaincy system. I remember we were staying in a hotel in Parramatta and it was time to vote again. Everybody wrote two names on a piece of paper and Tricia left the room to count them up.

'There's an overwhelming vote for one person,' she announced when she reappeared, adding that because of the result she was ditching the co-captaincy. That sole captain was me. The team was full of strong women who had far more experience than I did, yet they saw something in me. I felt myself going bright red. I was a terrible blusher. I had so little confidence, but I thought, wow, they want me to lead them.

Watching Kate recount that story, her sense of disbelief is still palpable. Probably because, like all of our journeys into elite sport, getting there is never easy. Maybe it's no accident that the one childhood memory seared into Kate's brain is of watching hurdles champion Sally Gunnell storm to victory in the 1992 Barcelona Olympics. She was twelve years old at the time.

It was the most incredible thing I'd seen in my life – just the raw emotion of her crossing the line and her flinging her arms up. You saw it all: the struggle, the pain, the relief and the pride was all there. And when the BBC played the slow-motion montage afterwards I remember thinking, Oh. My. God.

But for Kate, that struggle didn't begin on the hockey pitch; it began in primary school. She describes herself as a misfit, desperately trying to find her place. Born in the Manchester suburb of Withington, her parents Barbara and John were both PE teachers who encouraged her and her younger sister Rachel into sport at every opportunity. Eventually, it became the women in Barbara's hockey club, the Didsbury Greys, who provided Kate with a safe space where she began to flourish.

I got bullied a lot at primary school. I cut off my own fringe when I was seven and I had spiky hair and a mullet. And because I was doing lots of swimming and gymnastics I was naturally muscular with broad shoulders. I didn't fit in with what other girls looked like with their pigtails and dresses. And I had full lips, so kids called me 'monkey face' and other horrible, racist names. At school, it felt as though I was just surviving.

My sister and I always played sport through our parents,
but I don't remember much at primary school. We might get
the hoops out or chuck a few beanbags around, but I didn't
play hockey until I went to secondary school in Stockport.
Mum's team, Didsbury Greys, didn't have a junior section and
only boys could play at my dad's cricket club. There was also
lacrosse but, again, that was only for men.

When I did end up playing for Mum's team aged thirteen,
it was full of amazing women who were all really interesting
characters. Hockey is still amateur at club level so these weren't
only amazing women on the pitch; they were amazing off it too.
Some had families, some didn't, others were lawyers, doctors
or teachers and everyone came together at the weekend. These
were women comfortable being themselves. They were having
a good time. It was a happy place to be. They played together,
socialized together and laughed together. When they lost – and
they did – they were still together. I was an emotional person,
and I still am, and there was something about that emotional
connection that I loved.

Hearing Kate describe her formative experiences takes me back
to my own amateur team, Chester Hockey Club. At around
the same age, I would play with women of all stripes, some of
whom were pushing sixty. Admittedly, that felt intimidating for
me and similarly Kate remembers that while some adopted a
maternal role, others were all-or-nothing characters. It was also
an environment where women could be openly gay or bisexual

without judgement. From Didsbury Greys, Kate progressed to the Greater Manchester Under-16s before being selected for the North of England Under-16s. On that path, she was introduced to another woman who was to be a huge influence on her: Maggie Souyave. Every girl who trained in the north of England, including me, came across Maggie. Quietly spoken, but fiercely determined, she'd been a former England international before turning coach.

While Kate didn't find Maggie to be the best communicator, she could see she had a knack of driving players forward. A month or so after Kate turned sixteen, the Atlanta Olympics opened. Favourites to win, Australia's women's team – the Hockeyroos – oozed confidence and brought an athleticism to the women's game never seen before. Maggie handed Kate a VHS tape with the team's gold medal highlights. The timing was perfect. The agility and dynamism of the Hockeyroos had her hooked.

But before Kate could begin to emulate her new-found heroines, she had a wake-up call that turned out to be crunch time between coasting in regional hockey and propelling herself on to a national and international career.

Outside of hockey, I was still doing what every other kid my age did and that was drinking and hanging out in the park. By then I had trialled for the England Under-16s and been selected. I'd travelled to Santander and Inverness with the team but I was following my nose rather than actually doing anything to be better.

After I trialled for a second year, a letter arrived to say I hadn't been picked. I was shocked. The shame and embarrassment was overwhelming, like I'd let everyone down. I just wanted my mum to hug me but before she did, she said, 'It doesn't matter what we want or the coaches want. If you really care about this, you're going to have to make some decisions.'

After that, my parents took me on a 'summer of learning'. They arranged for me to do some assistant coaching in Bristol under Junior England coach Pete Atwell. It made me realize that he did value me as a player and person. They even took me to Milton Keynes to watch the tournament that I'd not been selected for. That was hard, but they wanted me to learn the lesson. I watched the matches knowing that while every girl deserved to be there and I wanted them to win, I didn't want them to win by too much. I was so conflicted and I cried all the way home.

Although you never recognize it at the time, it is experiences like that which define future sporting careers. Others may have given up, but Kate got her head down. She became a regular in the gym. She worked hard to improve her running and technical ability. She ditched drinking in the park and started to care about what she ate. But still, in her words, she was 'muddling along' hoping to take small steps up the ladder. Maggie Souyave stepped in again, only this time it left Kate speechless.

I remember sitting in a car with Maggie. 'What are your aims and ambitions?' she asked me. The conversation felt very serious. I must have been seventeen and I didn't know how the hell I was going to answer. 'I'm hoping to make it to the Junior World Cup this year and get to the Under-21s,' I replied. 'You need to think about the Sydney Olympics in three years' time,' she announced. Inside, I was laughing. It was such a mad thing to say. I thought, no way! But Maggie gave me that belief in myself. She was saying, don't just aim for what's in front of you. Go big. Go up here. Reach for the moon.

I know exactly that feeling. There is something about having the unthinkable spoken out loud that makes it become a crucial part of your journey. For me that happened quite late on in my career when in a tense one-to-one meeting the team coach, who I thought hated me, suddenly told me I was one of the world's best defenders. It gave me the confidence to focus and go for it on the pitch. But Kate also learned that adopting a single-minded attitude could be frowned upon if you were female – something that cropped up recurrently throughout her career.

I'll never forget someone saying to me late on, after I'd captained the England team for some years, 'You're obsessed.' And I knew that wasn't being said in a positive way. People have to appreciate that our male counterparts were being paid to play hockey full-time yet those professional hockey players were never labelled 'obsessed'. Women were still playing as amateurs. After I left college I was living at home and fitting in hockey alongside a university course in Liverpool. I had student loans coming out of my ears. I learned about focus from my mum and dad who had that mentality. Now I'm proud to be called obsessed.

In fact, Kate believes it was that obsession coupled with her ability to compartmentalize problems that coaches initially picked up on as perfect leadership qualities. This rang especially true when Kate's parents separated. Back then, instead of falling apart, Kate got on with the job, something she now believes was not altogether positive.

By that time I was training with the GB team and I was away a lot. The Sydney Olympics were coming up and I'd also started a relationship with Brett Garrard, who was on the men's team, and whom I was spending a lot of time with. I recall sitting in a stadium with my teammate Tina Cullen in Milton Keynes when I rang home. Whoever answered broke it to me that Mum and Dad were splitting up. I sat on the stairs and cried. And that was it. After that, I didn't talk about it. I had an ability to lock everything away. People said, 'Kate keeps going despite what's going on around her.' It was seen as a strength and a healthy way of dealing with pressure – a great leadership quality. Certainly, ploughing on can be beneficial at times, but it can also be very unhealthy. Thank God we've moved on.

In the end, Maggie's Sydney 2000 ambitions for Kate did come to fruition. She was selected, but in competition the team came a disappointing eighth. Yet I was surprised to hear that the qualities Kate developed were often born from similar failures. The Kate who captained me got respect because she held herself to the same high standards she demanded from everyone else. And what began to shape Kate's leadership style was the bitterest of starts to her captaincy. Eighth in Sydney was to be followed by much worse.

Following Sydney, Tricia Heberle stepped up from coaching the women's England seniors to coaching Team GB. What was seen as a positive move ended up being a baptism of fire. Only a few months into Kate being picked as captain, the women's team failed to qualify for the 2004 Athens Olympics. It was the first time we would not send a women's team since we first entered the games in 1988. Twenty years on, the devastation of that moment is just as raw for Kate. There are many reasons for team failure; some blamed it on decisions by the sport's governing body, England Hockey. Kate reveals that a breakdown of trust behind the scenes was also key to their ultimate failure. As a new leader, how did she make sense of it?

However shy or unsure I was off the pitch, I know I became a different person on it. I was able to use my voice, but now I understand that's such a small part of what it means to be a captain. I think much of our understanding of captaincy comes from the men's game – captains are put on pedestals, but real leadership is actually about every little thing, every single day.

In 2004 I allowed things to happen. I have no regrets because it's all I knew at the time, but I should have called out certain behaviours or had hard conversations with people. Things were going on that were unprofessional. For example, conversations that should have been confidential between players and staff weren't always kept that way.

I wasn't really conscious, or aware, of my responsibility. I had a small sphere of influence on the pitch and in how we trained. But I've since learned that teams are built through relationships. The trust you build between people is the most important thing, and a leader has an incredible role to play in that. Yes, as a captain you put the armband on, you do the speech in the changing room, and you go out and answer the difficult questions from the media, but it's mostly about the things that people don't see. It's about enabling and building. It's about challenging yourself and each other. It's about setting the example of the culture that you as a team are creating. That's a daily struggle, and it's a daily pressure to live by your standards and to be honest about things when you fail. You are put on a pedestal, but you're also human and have emotions.

That winning teams aren't shaped by what happens on the pitch is something I understand well. There are team cliques to navigate alongside personal rivalry: the fear that if you don't perform, there's always a better player ready to take your spot. Or the fear that if you speak out about a problem you may not get selected. For captains, it's a juggling act. Not only are they the bridge between players, but also the bridge between players, coaches and management – an obstacle course of personalities and styles to negotiate. Following Tricia Heberle's departure, a new coach Danny Kerry was appointed, a relationship Kate admits was never easy, but one that developed over time.

Perhaps we were too similar. I would go to Danny with a message from the team and he would react defensively and I would go away and get emotional. Then, I would do the same to him. It became like a dance. At the same time you can't let team members into those conversations, but it was exhausting. Yet I never felt like quitting as captain. I always knew it was going to be worth it because my values of fairness and justice for the team were so strong, and that overcame however hard any conversation would be.

In truth, challenging my teammates always felt far harder because that depended more on where I was in terms of my own playing. At times when I definitely had poor bouts of form it was hard to challenge others because I lacked confidence in my own ability.

Following the team's crushing exit from Athens, Kate led the players in writing a letter to Hockey England demanding a four-year dedicated GB women's hockey programme. In it, the team stressed they could no longer train part-time for ten months of the year and be expected to go out and win against teams playing full-time. Given that the women's team had just lost 70 per cent of its funding, it was a demand that ordinarily would have been logistically impossible, but for Kate it was an important statement of intent. Then, luck stepped in…

We'd put our marker down. We needed to change, but there wasn't the funding. But the timing turned out to be lovely. London's successful bid for the 2012 Olympics got announced in 2005. We'd have to bide our time, but we knew the money was coming. During that time, I developed a new respect for Danny and David Faulkner [England Hockey's performance director] because they started building a team off the back of nothing. After Athens, they took on a team that felt disheartened, angry and disillusioned – and we lost a lot of players – but we also had youngsters coming in and wanting a new way. After every Olympics there's a massive amount of transition and change, and it was a bumpy road.

The intervening years were to be a roller coaster for Kate off the pitch too. I was one of those youngsters who'd joined the GB team in the run-up to the 2008 Beijing Olympics. A fresh-faced nineteen-year-old, I got placed in the same room as Kate on a first trip away to Argentina. Just before the Games in Beijing, Kate and Helen Richardson, who were long-time friends, became an item. Kate finding herself in a lesbian relationship was a surprise even to her, she says, but she also now sees it as another crucial turning point in how she thought about leadership.

I'd known Helen since I was around sixteen. We were two kids in a hockey team but we became closer friends in the 2000s. In late 2007, I realized I wasn't happy in my relationship. I'd hit rock bottom, but once I decided what I wanted, the dust cleared. I thought, 'The most important thing is having a person in your life who gets you, who understands you, who listens to you and challenges you, whom you feel connected to and who wants the best for you. For me, that person was Helen. I'd never had feelings for another woman before, but I felt nothing but joy. Helen had been in front of me the whole time, and it was actually amazing.

No one knew about our relationship until the Beijing Games were finished. Helen and I shared a room and Rachel Walker [fellow midfielder] walked in. 'Are you two together?' she asked. After we confirmed it, we knew it wasn't going to be a secret for long and the team found out at the closing ceremony. Word started to get around and I remember some of the men's team not being particularly pleasant. That night we had a drink outside the GB apartments, and for the first time I found out what it felt like to be on the outside. Up until that point, I'd been a white, heterosexual woman from a middle-class background with all the privilege that that brought. Suddenly, I had the feeling of being 'othered'. It forced me for the first time to acknowledge discrimination in other forms. It allowed me to start seeing other people. I thought about racism or what it must be like in sport to be a woman with a disability. It started a process that fed into my own growth and development.

What Kate also realized, as many of us do, is how women in sport have put up with forms of discrimination, often accepting them as normal. It takes trailblazing women like US tennis superstar Billie Jean King, who has tirelessly campaigned since the 1960s for women's equal rights in sport, including pay and prize money, and more recently LGBTQ rights, to shift the dial. But what started for Kate as a question about sexuality kick-started other team conversations which Kate believes became crucial to the twelve-year process that led to us winning Olympic gold.

Because Helen and I were in the team together we had to start talking openly with Danny about our relationship. And he had to say to us, 'These are my concerns.' His biggest fear was that we'd break up and World War Three would erupt and we had to reassure him that our desire to take the team where it needed to go would override that. Each of us had to talk about our fears and not hide things away. Other women had identified as gay or bisexual before, but by us opening up I think it opened up another level to the team that became really healthy. We were vulnerable, but we were together.

After a poor performance in Beijing, Danny also knew he had to change his leadership style or lose us. He also went on a journey of self-development and he took us with him. It became a period of opening up and being vulnerable and creating safe spaces to help us become better. It definitely gave us a sense of responsibility, accountability and ownership. The leadership team, of which I was part, became part of the review process. We made decisions off the back of our conversations about team culture, and from those we established our vision and our values and our behaviours. And we also realized as a team we weren't good at having hard conversations.

I remember that period clearly and admittedly not all attempts at having hard conversations were successful. I'll never forget the 'circle of trust' that was trialled. At the time we were in Germany for a one-off Test match. Junior team members, like me, hadn't felt listened to and a weekly forum was set up so that players could air their grievances. The first time it was held, it was a tsunami of a conversation that went on well into the night. And afterwards players feared being ripped apart and the weekly sessions were dropped. For Kate it was a valuable lesson in 'growth mindset' – a technique based on developing self-awareness and awareness of others, but also about understanding failure and learning from it.

Leadership now is so much less about being autocratic and shouting in people's faces. It's about understanding different perspectives and thinking more broadly. It's about being genuinely connected to yourself and the people you are leading.

When you see people at the end of a session who have given everything of themselves but who are going through stuff in life, spending precious time together becomes so important. Everybody concentrates on the moment on the pitch when you

*win, but winning is actually about the time spent walking from
the training pitch to the car, and talking about something really
personal. It's about the coffee catch-ups. Those are the moments
when team cultures are made and broken. Those are the special
times that no one ever sees and no one ever talks about.*

*I saw all of this and more from the incredible group of
women that trained in the run-up to London 2012. Those
twenty-eight women really built, shaped and owned the culture
and absolutely laid the foundations for what was to come
in Rio. The medals we've won are of course important, but
honestly being part of this group really shaped me as a player,
leader and person.*

Winning team cultures are also never built overnight and Kate
believes that it took those years from 2008 to 2016 to get it
right – a period for the UK hockey team that wasn't without
its drama. Following a bronze medal win at the London 2012
Olympics and the departure of Danny Kerry as coach, the team
faced a new set of hurdles. In Danny's place came Jason Lee,
previous coach of the men's team. The women's team and Jason
got off on the wrong foot and the positive team culture that
had been slowly building turned toxic once more.

*When we moved to a centralized training programme in 2009
before the London Olympics, there were members of the men's
team who laughed at us. They said that training together full-
time was ludicrous. All the negative female tropes came out, like*

we'd be scratching each other's eyes out. Yet all the while, they were full-time hockey players. They were doing it, but we were the only ones branded as idiots. Jason Lee had been part of that and so when he came in as coach I knew he was from a mindset that didn't fully respect what we'd been building. Jason was a good coach, and the success and failure of a team never rests on one person, but there was a general lack of understanding about the importance of building team relationships. Now I think when a new leader comes in they need to listen, respect what's gone before and the people who have built it. They don't need to agree with it, but they need to respect it. There were some very hard meetings with Jason where we tried to explain what we were experiencing.

For me, personally, it became a slow burn after 2012. I felt the environment I was living and working in was wrong. The culture felt wrong, and I completely lost my way mentally and emotionally. One of my lowest points was at a Test match in San Diego having just been beaten by the USA. I remember coming off the pitch and hiding in the little dugout and just breaking down. I wanted so badly to make things better, but by 2014 I was in a very bad place. Unfortunately I didn't seek help until it was too late. I felt I was done.

So what made Kate stay on as captain? Why did she keep playing? What propelled her to become such an inspirational figurehead for players like me who weren't part of the behind the scenes but desperately wanted to win?

I think my ruthlessness came from failure. It came from the desire to want to win and not to fail. It wasn't until after we crashed out of the World Cup that the powers that be realized something needed to change and Danny came back to coach us. For the first time we put winning on the table as part of the conversation. You'd think that was obvious. Clearly everyone is there to win, but actually it became about what does winning mean? What's it going to take? We drilled down into every level of detail. We started to understand ourselves – what players looked like on a good day or a bad day, and if someone was having a bad day, how could we turn that around? Having that understanding of our differences, our strengths and weaknesses both on and off the pitch was massive. We cared about everybody's sense of self, and the change became incremental.

In sport, people always talk about marginal gains and it's usually technical, or scientific, but this was the psychological stuff. And there were uncomfortable moments. One time we each had to share what we thought our super-strength was. People are great at saying what they're poor at but to say 'I'm exceptional' is really hard. But we learned how to own it and through it we understood what everyone's super-strengths were and we created opportunities for them to deliver on those strengths. We had buddy groups and smaller spaces of discussion where people could develop bonds and be more intimate. There were spaces to listen and to be heard so that issues never got swept under the carpet. Often people want bold *changes and quick fixes but it's actually the everyday details that make all the difference and I believe it was a massive part of why we won in 2016.*

What culminated in Olympic gold in Rio was a culture I witnessed developing. In the end the team reached an understanding of each other where we didn't even have to use words. Whether it was during a game, or after a session, we could just look at one another and know what we were feeling or thinking. When it came to the tournament, I reckon most of us were playing at around 70 per cent of our ability, but our strength was that we'd found a level of consistency and a gut feel that Kate describes as an 'alchemy'.

I don't think any of it was necessarily conscious, but I think it's the most mindful we had ever been as a team. Every game felt like we were experiencing it in the moment. If you could bottle that and recreate it, it's about not being judgemental of what's happening; not thinking too much or too little; not thinking too much about what good or bad is, just facing each moment as it comes. That's when our play became really special.

Our first game against Australia was massive. They were medal contenders and we scraped it. But around three games in, I remember looking at Helen. We couldn't say it out loud, but we knew it was going well. We kept telling each other, one game at a time, and that forced us back to our routine and our rhythm. I think we all felt the momentum building, though.

We scored late and scraped our last pool game against the USA, but it gave us the confidence to go into the quarter-finals and annihilate Spain. Coming into the semi-final against New Zealand we defended with our lives and by the time we reached the final against the Netherlands it felt like we had nothing to lose. It was just amazing. But only a fraction of that win was about what happened that day. It was all the incremental stuff we'd built – the talking together, the getting up at 6 a.m. on a cold morning to train together, the positive culture, the being together, the losing together and the winning together. In that moment, under such intense pressure, we reverted to type.

CHAPTER 10

Digging Deep

Rebecca Adlington OBE

MIDDLE-DISTANCE SWIMMER

'I refuse to use filter apps. I don't want to be perceived as super-human. I'm human and I've achieved something and it's taken real sweat.'

In 2002 a thirteen-year-old Rebecca Adlington's parents took her to the Manchester Aquatics Centre to watch world swimming champion Ian Thorpe smash the 400-metre freestyle world record at that year's Commonwealth Games. The nineteen-year-old already had seventeen world records under his belt, but it was in front of crowds going wild that he beat his own world record of 3.40.17 by 0.9 of a second. The Australian swimmer, who had a unique lolloping style, left such an impression on the young Becky that from that day on her sporting trajectory was set. Yet she would have no clue where that journey might take her, or that at exactly the same age she would scoop two gold medals at the 2008 Beijing Olympics, going on to become Britain's most successful female swimmer.

I loved being in the water from day dot. If we ever went on holiday my mum would have to slap on so much sun cream my skin would turn yellow because I refused to come out of the pool all day. I felt so confident but when I was younger it was all about play. I'd never seen anyone who wasn't confident in the water. I have two older sisters, Laura and Chloe, and both of them could swim by the time I was born, so I never understood why I had to be in the baby pool with my armbands on. I wanted to be with my sisters and I'd follow them around, and when they joined a club I followed.

But I'll never forget being in Manchester watching Thorpe beat his own world record. The stands were packed and the noise was deafening. At that time the swimming world hadn't seen anything like it. His technique was phenomenal. Historically, distance swimmers have a messy technique because it's repetitive and you are covering more distance, but he had this lovely six-beat leg kick and really high elbows. I thought, this is what I want to do with my life.

Whether it's sprint or middle distance, swimming is one event I love to watch but just like Ian Thorpe twenty years ago, or the human flipper Michael Phelps who followed him, or Becky or today's superstar American Katie Ledecky, elite swimmers have that knack of making their sport look effortless. Certainly Becky was often presented as an everyday teenager who grew up in the small town of Mansfield in Nottinghamshire and whose talent was sometimes seen as God-given. Yet nothing could be further from the truth. Swimming is one of the most brutal physiological sports. The only way to win is to race many, many times, educating the body to tolerate extreme pain and building up enough mental resilience to push yourself to the limit. How did Becky get started and how did she discover her distance?

From swimming lessons and joining my local swimming club, Sherwood Colliery, I began competing around the age of nine and at ten I started competing more in individual races. In swimming the event chooses you, but you don't find that event until you are between thirteen and fifteen. I was never good at sprinting and there's a mix of reasons why certain swimmers are better at endurance. I've never been stick thin and that slowed me down from a speed perspective, yet it also gave me that ability to keep going over a longer period of time. But it's not always to do with height or size, even though most swimmers tend to be tall, broad-shouldered with no bum and bow legs. I also had very low lactic acid (the acid that is produced in the body to turn glucose into energy when oxygen levels decrease) and to be a good sprinter you need to be able to burn acid at maximum capacity. I just didn't have that capability. In distance swimming you are producing lactic but it never gets as high.

Having found her calling in middle-distance 400 and 800 metres, Becky's schedule became mind-blowing. I thought I was exhausting every hour at that age juggling between football practice and club hockey, but to fit in the 70,000 metres a week Becky needed to progress though the junior ranks took a dedication that singled her out from other teenagers. It was also the lengths to which her family went to support her that I find the most incredible.

Looking back, I don't know how we did it. I was training in Mansfield but when I needed to step up we found a club in Lincoln. It was around one and a half hours away. Mum and I would get up at 3 a.m. to get there. I would train for two hours, then I'd come back for school and she would take me again in the evening. Every day we spent up to four hours in the car. Mum did this for a whole year as well as caring for my two older sisters and working.

The first time I realized what an impact it was having on her was one time when she needed to pull over. She collapsed in the driver's seat and I had to bring her round. It wasn't just the hours she was driving. Mum is hard of hearing and she wasn't sleeping because she was so paranoid she wouldn't hear the alarm to wake me up for training.

That's when she said it was too much for her and we needed to find a club closer to home. That ended up being Nottingham's Nova Centurion club where I met my coach Bill Furniss. Even so, it was forty-five minutes away so we moved from a 3 a.m. to a 5 a.m. start. I ate my breakfast cereal from Tupperware containers on the way to school and dried my hair in the car air vent.

Becky's mum, Kay, was also proactive in applying for small council grants so Becky could travel for competitions or invest in a new swimsuit, but keeping all of those balls in the air took on epic proportions after Becky and her older sisters became ill. Chloe, who also swam, was forced to give it up completely after being diagnosed with chronic fatigue syndrome, or ME. Becky herself was diagnosed with post-viral fatigue after having contracted glandular fever without even realizing. However, most devastating was her sister Laura who was diagnosed with encephalitis – a rare inflammation of the brain caused by an infection. She spent months in hospital while Kay and Becky's dad Steve tried to keep some semblance of normality at home.

I didn't know I was ill because when you train like I did you constantly feel horrific – you are so tired from getting up early and swimming. Most of the time I could barely keep my eyes open. When I eventually went to the doctors they said I'd had glandular fever and that now I had post-viral fatigue.

Around the same time Laura got taken into hospital but my parents were very keen that I continue swimming. They wanted me to fulfil a passion but also have something to occupy me that was mine. I wasn't allowed to compete but I could still train so long as my heart rate was constantly monitored. But for Laura, there was a real possibility she might die.

At that point swimming became different for me. Whereas before I'd loved play and being in the water, it now had a calming effect on me. It became an escape. If I was happy I'd swim, and if I was sad I'd swim. It allowed me to work through my emotions. Unlike being in the gym where there is always something to distract you and I could feel on edge, with swimming I just switched off and let my mind wander. If ever I had a stumbling block, whether it was what was happening at home, or GCSEs or boyfriend break-ups, I would always come out of the pool with a plan.

When Becky was eventually allowed to resume competitive swimming, Kay and Steve then had another knife-edge decision to make. If Laura's condition took a turn for the worse and Becky was about to compete, would they tell her? It's a very tough call for any family of an elite sportsperson when another family member becomes unwell and it's a question that's asked of most athletes before going into major competitions. If a family member is taken ill or even dies, do you want to be told? After our winning final in Rio in 2016 I got told the news that my grandmother had suffered a stroke. My family decided not to tell me until after the game, which I believe was the right decision and thankfully my grandmother survived it.

But the choice is never clear-cut and it's always dependent on unique circumstances. I was interested to know how Becky approached the subject.

While Laura was in hospital I didn't see her. My parents didn't want my lasting memory of her to be hooked up to machines and now as a mum myself I understand that logic, but I did want to hold her hand and talk to her. It sounds odd, but in a way her being there helped me in sport. It gave me the realization that something was bigger. It helped me put everything in perspective. If I moaned I couldn't go fast in training because I'd been ill, I wasn't ill. My sister was ill. Nothing I did or didn't do was life or death.

When Laura eventually came out of hospital there was one occasion when she took a bad turn and had to be briefly readmitted. Mum and Dad had taken me to a junior competition and I knew something was up. I marched over and demanded they tell me but they hadn't wanted to because I was competing. I gave them a telling-off. Laura being ill never distracted from my performance, or had a negative impact. In fact, it was quite the opposite. Knowing helped calm my nerves. I told myself, 'Why am I stressing about swimming?' And if anything sudden had happened I probably wouldn't have competed. Swimming was my world but family is more important.

What also helped Becky during that period was having two great school friends who understood her training demands and planned time out to the cinema or a meal out around her one day off a week. She also had a solid group of swimming friends who were equally as supportive but didn't treat her with kid gloves, which also helped her focus. One of those friends was fellow swimmer and GB teammate Jo Jackson, whom Becky is still best friends with today. And in Becky's first Olympics in Beijing it was that close friendship that was to become pivotal to calming Becky's pre-competition anxiety. Amazingly, Becky's first Olympics was also the first competition she'd ever been to where she'd made a final. What were her expectations?

I never raced well mid-season. Everyone else went through hard training then performed well, but I always swam like I was swimming through custard. Instead, I raced well after I'd tapered and rested down (the period where swimmers decrease training volume before competition).

I competed in Rome just before Beijing. Everyone on the GB team raced well except me. I was awful. I came out of the race and my coach Bill said, 'What happened?' I told him, 'Fuck off.' He was a bit taken aback, but he took a moment and came back with, 'No, you fuck off.' We went round in circles for the next few minutes because we were so frustrated. When he eventually sat me down I broke down. I felt so much pressure. I'd only ever been to a World Championships before Beijing and never made a final. And I would start to feel nervous two months before a competition. He talked me through what to expect at an Olympics and suddenly it didn't seem so scary.

But I had no expectation of winning a medal and, rightly or wrongly, I'd compartmentalized the Games as a stepping stone for London 2012. Certainly Bill and I thought the best I could do was scrape a bronze in the 800 metres which was my strongest event. In the 400 metres we didn't even think I'd make a final.

So how did having her mate Jo there help? And how do two athletes suddenly switch off from being best friends to arch rivals in that intense moment of competition?

The night before I competed in the 400 metres I couldn't sleep. I couldn't eat. I had to eat energy gels for two weeks in the run-up to Beijing because I couldn't stomach real food. I thought I was going to cry and pass out.

Having Jo there was really beneficial. Coaches aren't allowed into the call room (the pre-race waiting room) and it's a horrible environment. There's usually a language barrier with the other competitors and everyone is psyching each other out. Some girls are listening to music on their headphones, but Jo and I sat and chatted. We chatted about anything other than the competition – hair, shoes, boyfriends – absolutely anything. When we got into the pool Jo was in the lane next to me and I was so grateful we were side by side. I think our friendship worked because neither one of us was dominant throughout our careers. If I wasn't on form I wanted her to win and vice versa. We'd both witnessed toxic environments at training camps and we decided that if we supported each other then the outcome would always be better.

I still remember so vividly watching Becky and Jo in that final and willing that Team GB would come back with a medal, but for Becky to come from nowhere into a winning position must have taken some digging deep. For that first 400-metre event her parents weren't even in the stands to cheer her on – the cost of coming to China for the whole week had been too prohibitive. Instead, they were due to arrive to support her in the 800 metres four days later. Knowing they would be at home cheering her on, she still remembers every metre of that race.

As soon as the starter signal went, all the girls shot off. I didn't find my rhythm and my stroke rate until the last 200, which was when the other girls were trying to hold on. Even so, I thought I'd come in around fourth. Jo was a full body length ahead of me and I didn't think I could catch up, but as it turned out she was dying a death. In the last 50 you can always hear the crowd cheering and the decibel level goes from 0 to 100 so you know it's getting exciting. It wasn't until I stopped and looked back at the clock at the other end that I saw I'd won gold. I had to look again. There's your name, then a gap, then your place and I didn't think I'd lined it up properly. It didn't feel real.

When I was younger if I ever dreamed of winning an Olympic medal then I'd pictured myself running around the pool naked cheering and celebrating. You never do what you think you are going to do. Instead it was the most bizarre thing in the world. And Jo had taken the bronze – we couldn't stop hugging. Both of us couldn't believe what had just happened.

Did that unexpected success help Becky four days later when she had to go out and swim the 800 metres? Her coach Bill Furniss described her stroke as 'economical, strong, perfectly balanced and fluent', but to win, all of that and more has to come together on the day. How did she put all that disbelief and elation in a box and refocus?

On the podium I forgot to sing the national anthem. I was busy watching my team in the stands and looking at Jo and thinking about my next race. I needed to swim down, get my massage, go to doping control. In my head I had so much to do. When I got back to my room, I put my medal in my drawer and I didn't get it out until after the 800 metres. I also needed to get away from the energy of the village. There was a quiet pool Team GB had access to but no one used, so I trained there.

When it came to the day, I felt ready. I felt so confident. Usually Bill and I talked tactics on the way to the call room, but it's the only time in my career when I stopped him and said, 'I'm ready.' He said, 'Okay.'

When I dived in, I went for it. It felt effortless. Unlike the 400 metres I didn't have to get into it. Eight minutes of pain is never easy, but I felt the ease of how I thought an Olympic final should feel.

Whenever I breathed I could see Bill. He was going mental and I thought someone was chasing me, so I put my head down and pushed on. Everything was on fire by this point: my shins, my ear lobes. The lactic acid was just racing around me. Then my stomach muscles started cramping. My stomach was in bits and I was terrified I was going to throw up or something even worse. I thought, I can't let this happen at an Olympics! When I stopped my whole body was vibrating because I'd pushed it to such a limit. It was sheer pain, but I knew it was my last race. I didn't care. I just kept pushing and pushing.

Not only did Becky smash her second gold, but when she touched the wall at 8.14.10 she shaved 2.12 seconds off a world record set by American Janet Evans nineteen years earlier. She also became the first woman to win gold for Great Britain since the swimmer Anita Lonsbrough in 1960, as well as becoming the first British swimmer to have won multiple golds since Olympic swimmer Henry Taylor in 1908.

Becky was to meet Anita Lonsbrough on a couple of occasions after Beijing, but she admits that she would have liked a female role model and a confidante for the modern age who may have helped her handle the next stage of her career. At nineteen years old, in 2008 Becky had become a household name overnight just at a time when sports personality and celebrity culture was starting to explode, helped by the rise of social media.

Anita was absolutely lovely, but I met her after Beijing and I found it hard to connect her experience to mine. When she won gold it was 1960 and there wasn't the press intrusion or social media or celebrity culture and those were the things I found hardest to navigate. Even Bill didn't feel he could coach me. He was honest and said he didn't have the experience to coach a double-gold Olympic champion. The pressure is very different.

It was actually the cyclist Chris Hoy who stepped in to help me deal with a lot of the attention I got. After we landed back in the UK, no one had explained to me there would be open-topped bus tours and hours of interviews or that I'd go to Buckingham Palace, and school visits. I went along with all of it but I really struggle to remember any of that period. I was knackered. Chris was the one who said to me, 'Becky, you don't have to say yes to it all. You are going to kill yourself.'

While much of the attention celebrated Becky's stunning achievements, she was also catapulted into the harsh reality that not all of it was going to be positive. By becoming the only poster girl of female British swimming, she experienced a dark side to women's sport that I personally despise along with so many other sportswomen I know. We can carry off the most stellar performances on the pitch, in the pool or on the track, but we are still judged on how we look. Even after we've stopped competing and our bodies have changed shape through ageing or after we've had kids, people feel they have a right to comment. Yet for me, women pursuing an active lifestyle in everyday life or competing professionally represent beauty in its purest form. I wanted to know how Becky coped with that criticism and how she feels about it more than a decade after her retirement?

I was being criticized over things that men weren't. There were stories about my appearance and what I was wearing, but men were only being judged on their performance. Had there been a Katie Ledecky around who had been a role model closer to my age who had experienced all of that, then perhaps I would have sought advice from her, but there wasn't.

It felt awful, but it also felt weird. At school there were girls who would go for a night out with crimped hair and full make-up, but I dried my hair in the car air vent. At swimming you could see everyone's imperfections, all their lumps and bumps and cellulite and no one cared. I had acne as a teenager which maybe dented my confidence, but at swimming no one cared if you had a spot. No one wore make-up or concealer. We all swam when we were on our period. We used a tampon and got on with it. Looking good was about whether we were in great swimming shape.

Now I refuse to use any filter apps or airbrushing across any of my social media. It's not normal and it's damaging to girls. Sometimes people say to me now, 'Oh, you're prettier than you look on TV.' Or, 'You're not as big as I thought you were.' But I'd rather look better in real life than online, and I don't want my online persona to bear zero resemblance to me,

or for my daughter to see two different people. I don't want
to be perceived as super-human. I'm human and I've achieved
something and it's taken real sweat which is what you need
to win gold medals. But, I won't lie. There are times when I
don't want to go out on the red carpet because I don't want
to worry about what people might say. I still struggle with the
scrutiny. But I also tell myself, who cares about what people
think of my stomach or my arse? It's not life or death and I
have people around me whose opinions I value much more.

When it came to her sport, it was the pressure of expectation
post-Beijing that was also to affect Becky in the lead-up to
London 2012. So much rested on her shoulders, and I can
only imagine the burden she must have lived with. In 2010, a
couple of years after her gold medal win in Beijing, she says
she experienced what we call 'choking'. It's a phenomenon
whereby pressure and anxiety leads athletes to over-think and
analyse processes that previously came automatically and it
can lead to a drop in performance. For many it can be hard to
bounce back from. Maybe it's no surprise now that Becky is a
fantastic advocate for promoting positive mental health as well
as physical health. At the elite level the two go hand in hand.

I reached a point where I didn't like racing the 800. It's an
extremely hard race. It's brutal on your body and it was taking
me a week to recover from racing. I felt like I'd been in a fight
every time. And I really struggled with motivation because I

thought I was never going to achieve what I did in Beijing. It felt out of reach. There was an expectation that I was always going to win and beat a world record. I continued training but I felt stale and stuck.

I got a sports psychologist after Beijing because I also became very stressed about race outcomes. I worried that a rival was going to swim faster than me. I worried what would happen if I lost. I worried about everything. He said I needed to focus much more on the journey. He told me, 'Becky, all you are doing is putting your hat and goggles on and going for a swim.' Just like my sister's illness had helped me put everything in perspective before, it had the effect of calming those voices in my head.

Becky also travelled to Australia to the Gold Coast for two months to train, which helped her switch off some of the negative feelings she was experiencing. British Swimming supported her and she says the change of scene gave her the spark back to tackle London 2012. This time around, in her early twenties she was able to take the event more in her stride. However, by then, swimming itself had also altered course and Becky came away with two bronze medals, beaten in the 400 metres by France's Camille Muffat and in the 800 metres by Katie Ledecky, who went on to dominate in the sport and is still smashing records more than a decade later.

The sport had got faster. Distance swimmers like me who had competed in the 800 metres were more likely to also compete in the 1500 metres. At the sprint end, swimmers who ordinarily took on the 100 metres and the 200 metres were taking on the 400 metres. The sport was changing and I fell into this weird bracket of being a 400-metre and 800-metre swimmer. I also had a shoulder injury. My shoulder was hanging on by a thread. I was in physio twice a week and living off painkillers. Every time I breathed it pushed my shoulder higher and it was incredibly painful. Going into 2012 I knew I wasn't going to win, but I could never come out and say that. Although I didn't announce it until the next year I'd also made the decision to retire after 2012. With hindsight maybe I shouldn't have thought about the decision until after the games, but my team knew it.

Now I think to get a bronze in both the 400 metres and the 800 metres was a phenomenal achievement. I didn't expect a medal in the 400 metres at all but I did expect to do better in the 800 metres. There will always be that disappointment and I think it's why I couldn't stop crying on the podium. For a few reasons, it was very emotional.

It's hard enough in a situation like that to channel your own disappointment, but at times Becky again also found herself channelling the opinions of a nation. While so many people understood her journey and supported her, others contacted her over social media to tell her how she'd let people down. These days I get so angry at social media pile-ons on to young athletes who do phenomenally well, but may not go on to repeat that success immediately or ever again. Outside of sport, it's hard to comprehend the strain on teenagers like Becky and more recently athletes like Emma Raducanu following her US Open tennis win in 2021. How did Becky find the strength to deal with it?

At the time it was very difficult to get those messages. What made it harder was that I was disappointed, but it was only me and my coach who had the right to be disappointed. I had to digest that grief and I didn't need people's opinions. I cried for forty-eight hours. I was heartbroken because I knew I was better.

But now I think about it differently, and this is even a controversial subject among sportspeople. There's one camp who believe there should only be gold medals. I had fellow teammates who believed that you'd lost the gold if you'd won silver or bronze. However, I'm in the camp that thinks an Olympic medal of any colour is a phenomenal achievement. Everyone wants gold, but a silver or bronze is still a win and it's extremely difficult. You've got more chance of being hit by lightning than winning an Olympic medal.

But you still have to grieve it. You'll never have that moment back and you have dedicated every single waking moment to it. It's not just the 70,000 metres in the pool I did every week. It's every waking hour. Even in your switch-off time you are thinking about how that will impact performance. I'd dedicated four years to that moment, but in reality I'd dedicated fifteen years of my life to it. It's not something you get over easily and it takes time.

For the record, I'm definitely in Becky's camp and couldn't agree more. But Becky hasn't just proved herself to be an Olympic star. Having retired at twenty-three, Becky launched herself into setting up her own swimming programme with the aim of getting every child to swim 25 metres by the time they leave primary school. At her swim centres children don't only learn swimming, they are encouraged to be good friends, to be respectful and to be determined – all the qualities that Becky developed from swimming with her sisters aged three to becoming an Olympic champion sixteen years later. With two young children herself she rarely has time to swim these days, but vows to get back to it. She absolutely loves her sport, she tells me. So, what was her most memorable moment?

After my 800 metres win in Beijing I had loads of press to do, but our daily team meeting was at 4 p.m. I got back to the Olympic village at 3.50 p.m. but I hadn't eaten any solid food in days, only energy gels. I ran to McDonald's, grabbed a burger and ran to the meeting. I was late by around five minutes. Lateness was never allowed and I knew I was going to get a real bollocking. But when I walked in the whole team stood up and gave me the biggest round of applause. It was one of the best moments of my career. Their respect and their opinion meant everything to me. These were people who knew me, understood me and knew how hard it was. It meant the absolute world. It felt so special.

CHAPTER 11

Conquering Expectations

Christine Ohuruogu MBE

400 METRES SPRINTER

'I was devastated to leave home. It's where I learned to succeed, but I had to leave the chaos and start seeing myself as an elite athlete.'

It was following the London 2012 Olympics that 400-metre sprinter Christine Ohuruogu published two children's novels aimed at girls. In her *Camp Gold* series, Maxine is a schoolgirl who discovers a talent for running and sets out on a path to win Olympic gold. If any of that sounds familiar, then it is. Maxine, like Christine, is an ordinary girl who got inspired and found herself on an unexpected sporting journey, bumping up against some tough challenges along the way. For Christine, whose own career hit jaw-dropping highs as well as some agonizing chapters, it's a tale so many sportswomen can relate to. And like all of us, it wasn't in the world's stadiums where Christine's dreams were built. It was the local parks and recreational grounds around where she grew up in East London – an area that was to become the home of the 2012 Olympics – that sparked her imagination.

For me, sport was about a sense of adventure and challenge, and about pushing myself. Publishing those books was about trying to show girls that yes, there's the Olympics, but I didn't grow up with any of that stuff, yet I still wanted to make something of myself. And the parks near home shaped that love for activity and adventure. Later in school, I started developing myself in organized sports, but that initial love came from running around them [the parks] or playing out in the streets. I didn't do it because I believed there was a future in it for me, or because I wanted to be an Olympic champion. I didn't know about any of that – to me I was just enjoying the freedom of being outside.

When I talk to Christine, she still bubbles with all the energy and enthusiasm that she had when, aged twenty-two, she first burst on to the international athletics scene back in 2006, winning a Commonwealth gold in Melbourne. Yet I am to discover her story has far more to it than I knew. Behind her winning smile was a teenager who pushed herself to the extreme in every way and who placed on her shoulders a weight of responsibility:

not just throughout her sporting career, but at home where she was the eldest girl in a large family of eight children. Organized chaos reigned in the Ohuruogu household, she tells me, but life had to carry on regardless.

I didn't start out as one of eight when I was a kid. My older brother and I are the oldest out of the bunch which meant we were around to watch the other kids being born. When it was just the two of us, everything got split down the middle, then every couple of years we would begin to feel the squeeze: things were split into thirds when my brother came, then quarters with the arrival of my sister and so on.

My parents were first-generation Nigerian and Dad was a chief marine engineer and was away from home frequently. That meant Mum needed an extra pair of hands. As the oldest daughter, I shouldered much of that caring responsibility growing up. As a family, we had to function. We had to keep moving. We had to keep the household going every day despite setbacks. From a young age I understood the power of being responsible, and the power of setting a good example. That weight of expectation was something that was planted deep in me as a child.

I myself grew up in a small house as one of four children. That felt cramped enough, and I remember our back garden being the place where all kids gravitated to, especially me and my twin brother Shaun because we loved to play football. We put up goalposts and Shaun's mates would come over for a game until we began playing at local clubs. For Christine it would be the streets and parks that became so integral to her journey. Holidays for a family of ten would have been prohibitively expensive, she explains. Instead, impromptu street-meets and vital community sports programmes filled that gap.

We had a lot of fun. It was pretty chaotic, but I loved the fact that we were very active. We didn't spend a lot of time watching TV. We had friends on our street, and we'd spend evenings playing out. There was football, but we also had roller skates or we raced around on our bikes or we'd tie a skateboard to a bike and pull it. When you raced around the corner you'd have to try hard not to lose your balance and fly off the skateboard!

Our house was between two parks. One was a recreation ground, and the other was West Ham Park – a huge park. In the summer it ran a free play scheme. When I look back now I think it was such a wonderful gem for the area. Open play schemes like that don't happen any more. You could just walk in off the street and register with your parents' permission. Our summer holidays were mostly spent at home, but we still had the ability to be outside during the summer whether it was rain or sunshine. I have such fun memories of summers at the play scheme. One time I actually beat my older brother in a 400-metre race that we had organized amongst ourselves when I was around nine; we laugh about it a lot now despite his embarrassment at the time that his little sister beat him in front of his friends.

And that was also the great thing about having an older brother. As a girl I was never discouraged from joining in. In fact, everything he did I was expected to do and probably do it better than him. If he got good grades I should do as well as him or better. If he played sport, it was the same.

For Christine, sporting heroes or heroines weren't those seen on TV every four years, although funnily enough she was nicknamed Linford Christine at primary school. The British-Jamaican Olympic sprinter Linford Christie had become a household name during the 1992 Barcelona Olympics when Christine was eight. Instead, Christine's real sporting journey started when she picked up a book in her school library.

I was such a boffin and I was always in the school library catching up with my homework. I remember picking up a book on netball which had a picture of the England team in it and I thought, 'That's what I want to do – play netball for England.' I was playing for my secondary school team and had no knowledge of how I would even get to the England team, but the seed had been sown.

As I was an academic child, my parents never objected to me doing sport so long as my grades stayed up. I had smart friends and I was pushed academically, but I also sat in the sports camp which I loved being a part of. Sport worked well for me in a way I could never have imagined. I know that it is sport that pulled me out of my shell and helped me develop a strong sense of self-assuredness which was important as I was never very confident growing up. And in between my studies and my sport I was also coming home and doing all of my household duties. I wasn't dropping any balls.

That Christine started off in one sport – netball – and then found her true calling in another is a path I'm familiar with. I started off loving my football before trying hockey and then running my training alongside. I seemed to take to hockey naturally and wanted to continue playing throughout secondary school. For me, playing team games tapped into my love of shared experiences – I performed well when I had a specific job to do, and there was something about sharing accomplishments that also appealed to me. Even now I love being part of a team on *Question of Sport*. But for Christine to gravitate from a team sport to an individual pursuit is unusual, so I was interested in what ignited her passion for track and field. The answer, she tells me, was pure accident.

Athletics were part of school lessons and we did inter-form competitions. Everyone got to pick the event they wanted but, typical me, I let everyone pick before I did. I was prepared to take what was left which was the 800 metres. I'd never run anything close. And I didn't know much about athletics distances, either. I remember thinking, 'Goodness me! What exactly is 800?' The teacher told me it was twice around the track. I practised at lunchtimes and when it came to the race,

I won it. And I don't know how I did, but I won it by loads.
All that practice paid off.

When I finished, my form teacher asked, 'Christine, have you
ever been coached?' Unlike netball where there are discernible
skills like catching and pivoting, I didn't think you needed a
coach for running. A classmate overheard our discussion and
he told me to look up the Newham and Essex Beagles Athletic
Club in the Yellow Pages which was the club he trained at. It
was a great idea for me: if I improved my running I could get
better at netball. That was my primary concern as I played in
defence, but I'd always wanted to play in my dream position of
centre. In my mind, running quicker was the key. When I found
the Newham and Essex Beagles I rang them up and told them
I wanted to join. That's how I started on my athletics journey.

Like me, Christine was also to discover that if she was to pursue
either sport to a senior level, some tough calls needed to be made.
I had the heartbreaking decision at sixteen to choose between
football and hockey. I chose hockey and I'll never forget having
to make the phone call to the coach at Tranmere Rovers, where
I played, to tell her I was leaving the women's football team. I
still have moments when I think of where I'd be if I'd chosen
differently. Having worked her way up in netball and been invited
to join an England international programme, Christine was
faced with the same agonizing choice. Her schedule had become
dizzying. Alongside her studies and her duties at home, much of
Christine's time was spent on public transport. Her school was in

Romford in Essex – an hour away on the bus. Her regular routine would be to attend school, travel home, get changed, jump on a bus to get to netball practice or running practice, and this would happen most nights of the week with club and county matches played on weekends. What drove her, I wondered?

I kept all the plates spinning and looking back it was a mad mess, but there was a routine to the madness. I made it work. I was committed to my netball team, but my coach at Newham and Essex Beagles, a man called John McEwan, believed in me. He kept telling me, 'Christine, you can do this.' He was coming in from Essex to coach me and a couple of others. He was really making the effort to commit to us.

He was especially proud because not long after he began coaching me I made an international appearance for Team GB in France. The event itself was terrifying. Suddenly I was by myself. I don't think I slept the whole trip because I was so scared. I remember as soon as I got off the plane, the fear consumed me. Even driving from the airport to the hotel I was scared, and from the hotel to the first competition I was scared. I don't know how I got around that race. I didn't think I would get round in one piece. I was also the new person on the GB team. Everyone knew one another. I thought they'd be watching me and judging me. This wasn't club competition any more. It was international level – the stuff you see on TV. When I came third, there was such a sense of relief: 'Thank God it's over. I crossed the line. I'm still alive.'

Afterwards I felt compelled to keep training, but it's funny because no one told me I had to do it. No one told me I had to run helter-skelter from one sport or activity to the next. No one was forcing me. I did it, firstly, because I loved sport and secondly, I knew my hard work would pay off somewhere down the line. And it always did.

Christine juggled netball and sprinting for as long as she could, but it was when John moved further into Essex and couldn't travel in to coach her that she switched running clubs to nearby Mile End. There she was coached by Lloyd Cowan (assisted by Kevin Park) whom she was to stay with for the whole of her international career, but it was also there that she reached breaking point. In 2003 she won bronze in the 400 metres at the European Junior Championships. It was her first international championship, and having never realized her dream position of centre in netball, it sealed her future.

So, how did it feel for Christine to have been surrounded by teammates going through the highs and lows of winning and losing, to suddenly being thrust out on to the track on her own? Admittedly, I would have found it almost impossible because even in teams where personal relationships are fraught, when you get out on to the pitch you all support one another to win.

The Euro Juniors was my first taste of a proper championship, and I loved the freedom of it all – running and getting into the spirit of athletics. Preparing on my own was scary, but my teammates were never too far away. When I won the bronze, the feeling was out of this world. I was the slowest on the start list for the final, yet my strength got me over the line to clinch my bronze. I didn't feel like I had 'made it' or that the sport was my calling, but I knew I had taken an important step in raising my confidence in a new sport.

But the truth was I never had a sense that I was great at anything. What I did know was that I was good at working hard and pushing myself. That was my saving grace. Lloyd said I was good as an athlete but at that point I still thought of myself as a netballer – I was caught between the two. When I was invited to join the England netball camp, Lloyd said he couldn't keep losing me to weekends of netball training. I had to make a choice. Making that phone call to the England women's head of performance to tell her I was quitting was hard. Netball was my dream. I loved it and I was quitting for something I didn't know was going to work. It was a huge risk and I was acting on a wing and a prayer, but that was my love for adventure.

That the 400 metres also became Christine's race also fascinates me. It's a distance I love watching because of the heart-pumping, on-the-edge-of-your-seat rush, but it's also notoriously hard – arguably one of the most physically demanding track events because athletes have to maintain a faster time over a longer distance than in any other sprint.

In Olympic competition, women were banned from racing

the 400 metres until 1964 when it first appeared on the programme. Like so many other running events, it was deemed too strenuous. Running it also requires the body to produce enough lactic acid – the substance your body creates to break down glucose for energy when it starts running out of oxygen – to sustain a runner over the distance.

Christine famously became known for having a 'late burst' which looked to spectators as though she left it nail-bitingly last minute to step up her pace and cross the finish line. And while she is not an athlete to do anything by halves, I wanted to know what it took out of her physically and mentally every time she ran.

The 400 metres is a horrible event, but I loved it. It's an elongated sprint and there are different ways to explain it technically, but I like to break it down into 200 metres and 200 metres. In the first 200 metres I needed to be running near enough within a second of my maximum speed. So, you've already pushed yourself to 90 per cent and then you have to try and hold that for the second 200 metres. From that point onwards you're delving into some deep, deep lactic. It's really intense anaerobic work and as your body is basically running out of oxygen, everything in your body is screaming from 200 metres on. There's blood rushing around and you're thinking, 'Why am I doing this to myself?'

It always looked like I had a last-minute burst, but that was never the case. It was an illusion. While the other athletes were slowing down I was maintaining my speed. I was good at keeping even-balanced 200 metres. For the first 200 metres, it looked like I'd gone off 'slow', but I hadn't. I've gone off within my 90 per cent max of running and I just managed to hold my pace very well, and that's where my strength lay.

The race is also a gruelling test of mental strength and where you are placed in the starting lanes also becomes a crucial element in your judgement, Christine explains.

Mentally the 400 metres is very tough. You must run at a pace that is completely your own, and it is very easy to get that wrong when you are running at speed, with very little time to think.

The first challenge is where you are positioned on the track. Runners start at a different spot, either slightly behind or ahead of other competitors. Because of that stagger it creates a false perception that if someone is ahead, then you must be far behind. It can lead you to misjudge your speed. Trying to figure out which pace is your best pace despite what everyone else is doing is hard. It's just you and your mind deciding what that safest pace is, and you have to trust you have got it right.

At 300 metres where everything levels out, the race for the line begins and the chase is on. Everyone hopes that they have enough left in the tank to either hunt down their rival who is ahead or flee from their rival on their heels and hold on to the lead. The last 100 metres feels like a lifetime of running. The pain increases as it seems like the line pulls further and further away. You hear the excitement of the crowd along with the blood roaring in your ears, and tunnel vision sets in as you focus squarely on what is ahead. The legs are heavy, your chest is burning and you are thinking, 'Where is the line?'

No matter how tough the race, having discovered her calling I wondered whether Christine missed team sports, and how she mentally coped with her new sporting landscape.

In team games you can be brilliant, but if you don't suit the script of play in that moment you won't get played. In athletics, I loved the experience of being on my own, setting my own goals, and having that ability to work for myself and get a result. However, there was also a lot of naivety: I had no idea of expectations or what the standards of performance were. Now when I look back, I think that was a good thing. Unlike my coaches I had no vision of it. I wasn't brought up with a sporting mind so I didn't know the extremities of good or bad. I was just happy to turn up and have a good session. I laughed my way through everything: I loved it. I was just enjoying myself.

Winning the bronze medal at the European Juniors confirmed to me that athletics was the best place for me, and with more training I knew that I would be in a better position for the following year, which happened to be the Athens Olympics. It was tentative, but I thought, 'If I can train a bit harder, maybe I can get on the relay team and get to the Olympics.' I had no real idea of what that entailed but it didn't matter. What was important was that I had a goal. I had a target.

That strategy paid off. Christine did make the Athens Olympics, reaching the semi-finals in the 400 metres individual event and being part of the relay team who came fourth in the 4 × 400 metres final. But it was over the next couple of years that Christine's star truly began to rise. At the 2005 World Championships she won a bronze medal as part of the women's 4 × 400 metres relay team, and the following year clinched her gold in the 2006 Commonwealth Games in Melbourne.

But right at that moment, as she moved towards the peak of her career, everything was to come crashing down around her. During all of this, she was still living at home with her family, still caring for her siblings and now juggling a university degree as well as part-time work. This led to her missing three drugs tests and being banned for one year from competition. At the time, a new system for testing had been introduced which required athletes to register their whereabouts so testing agencies could conduct unannounced visits. Nowadays, 'whereabouts' is common in athletes' vocabulary, and technology is now available via apps which enable information regarding where an athlete is going to be located at any given time to be updated quickly and easily. However, none of that existed in Christine's era. Instead, many athletes faxed in their whereabouts.

As a result of the one-year ban, a lifetime ban from Olympic competition also loomed over her. Why did she miss her tests and what impact did that devastating ruling have on her?

The whole experience was really quite traumatic and it still affects me to this day. I accept I did do something wrong. I missed three tests. But what was difficult is that I could understand the context behind it. The arbitrators could also understand but the rules were the rules. The new system sounded very straightforward in theory, but life takes over. I was still living at home with my multitude of siblings and I didn't want drug testers testing me at my home because the only possible time they could come was first thing in the morning. At that time it was pure chaos: brothers and sisters were going to school, college or university, and my parents were going to work. There was one bathroom at the time. I didn't feel I could expose anyone to the madness of my home; it would have been an awkward logistical nightmare! So I chose riskily to rely on my training venues, but that meant I had to be there when I said I was going to be and of course I had every intention of doing so.

Again, in theory that was fine. But with the changing availability of the athletics facilities along with my coach not working full-time, there was a lot of chopping and changing leading to the unfortunate result of missing the random tests. The shock of the fallout propelled me to change my lifestyle. I had to be professional, otherwise I was letting my talent down.

Seeing yourself as an elite athlete can be a very hard transition to make, and it's also something I've had to deal with in my career. To realize your dreams you have to start being selfish. In a period when I hadn't been picked for the international squad several times over, I moved out of the flat I was sharing with two teammates and rented a one-bedroom flat. I focused on my training, my diet – everything that would make me a better athlete. Christine had a similar decision to make, but it came with the added weight of being a primary carer in her family – a factor that is seen as one of the main barriers to all women pursuing sport or having an active lifestyle. For the elite athlete it has life-changing ramifications.

After the decision, I knew I had to leave home, but I was devastated to leave home. It's where I learned to succeed, but I had to leave the chaos and start seeing myself as an elite athlete. What was also devastating for me was I did so much for my brothers and sisters. I thought when I left everything was going to fall apart. I thought deep down they would think ill of me, like I was abandoning them and I was not interested in their lives any more. The guilt overwhelmed me as I was my mum's second pair of hands. I tried to move out a first time but couldn't; I sat in the car and cried. I wasn't ready to leave. By the second attempt, I was ready and I made sure I didn't move far away so they could come round. Moving meant I could have my drugs tests done at home. I knew I had to protect my career and I never missed a test after that.

It's not just the change in mindset and lifestyle that Christine had to come to terms with. It's also the reputation damage that any link to perceived doping might have. Sadly, I know only too well. In 2008 I was prescribed an inhaler which could have saved my life on the pitch due to diagnosed asthma. While I legally carried it, the accompanying certificate it needed became the focus of a computer hack on the World Anti-Doping Agency database in 2016 which 'outed' twenty-six athletes, including me. Although I knew it was a pathetic attempt to smear not just me but the whole GB gold medal hockey team, I constantly worried what damage it might do to my 100 per cent clean record and also how my family and friends might be affected. What impact did it have on Christine?

It was written in the rules that the story had to go to the press. And I knew that once it went public, my life was over. It wouldn't matter what the details of my case were, nobody was going to care. Once you have any story concerning anti-doping, it doesn't matter what the context is. It doesn't matter that you forgot. It doesn't matter that you have a chaotic life. I could see what others would see: a black, immigrant family with an unpronounceable surname with loads of kids growing up in East London. I knew the story was ripe for bias and that's what happened. My dad was mortified because my parents are well-educated people and he was a proud, upstanding man. People were calling him from Nigeria as the news had blown up. All he kept asking me was, 'Christine, what has happened?'

After the news had broken I spent days in bed. I couldn't get up. I was twenty-two at the time and nothing in the years of my upbringing came even close to what I was experiencing. It was very tough. Having grown up with the weight of expectation, I knew this fell far below what was expected of me. I was a big sister. I took that job very, very seriously. I did everything right. My parents had worked very hard and it wasn't for me to destroy everything. This was a failing on such epic proportions that I blamed myself. I was always the one fixing stuff, but I couldn't fix this – no one could. It's only now when I look back that I can forgive myself, because in everything that I did, I was always trying to do the best that I could to keep things working for everyone else, and in that I had unfortunately given myself too much to do.

That Christine got back on the track at all is amazing to me, but she credits her team with gradually encouraging her – a sporting family who believed in her unquestionably and kept turning up to work with her even when she didn't want to return to the sport. Having lost her funding, a kind benefactor stepped in and provided enough money to keep her training, even though the rules of the ban didn't allow her to compete. At the time, Christine was also becoming plagued by injury – in particular both of her Achilles tendons. After double surgery she gave herself the best chance of returning to competition, but physical rehab is only one part of the equation. I was interested to know how she regained her motivation.

I wanted to rehab my legs so I could still run and the surgery went well. My team were still intact. They turned up and got me to work. It gave me such a deep respect for everything they did to get me back. It was so heart-warming to know there were people in sport who understood and said, 'Chris, we get you.'

I also had a job to do. I couldn't keep investing energy into what people might or might not be thinking about what had happened. I had a coach cracking a whip at every opportunity to get me going and I had a team working so hard to get me back up and running. I needed to make something good come out of the mess that I found myself in. I had many people cheering me on, through kind words, phone calls, prayers. It was immense and I felt incredibly humbled that people were willing me on.

Christine didn't just turn it around, she turned things around spectacularly. She won World Championship gold in Osaka in 2007 before taking gold at the Beijing Olympics in 2008, beating pre-race favourite Sanya Richards and recording the fastest time that year of 49.62 seconds. In the intervening years between that and the London Olympics in 2012, injury continued to plague her, but at her home games she took silver at the Queen Elizabeth Olympic Park in the stadium so close to where she had realized her dreams as a child. What did that medal mean to her?

When I took gold in Beijing it felt like redemption, but London was different. It was my home. It meant everything to me. Although I went in with a view to win and defend my title, I am genuinely proud to have got silver. There is a lot of should have, could have, would have. But I had a lot of respect for Sanya Richards-Ross who took gold.

Sometimes I forget the four years that went before that, and I think to have got back to the level I was at in 2008 and competed on my home turf, that was something special and I should never lose sight of that. When I look back on my career now, I'm lucky to have lasted for so long. The 400 metres takes its toll and not many athletes get the fifteen years of quality running I did.

Christine eventually retired in 2018 and now sits on the board of GB Boxing as well as pursuing a career in law. She applied after seeing the position advertised for an elite athlete and she wanted to understand sports governance. As boxing is an individual sport, there were also similarities between it and athletics and she felt her knowledge was transferable. As one of the few women from a black ethnic minority background in a position of influence in sport, I wondered how important it is to her that diverse voices are heard at every level and how her own experience has shaped how she's approached different roles.

Track and field is split evenly down the middle between males and females. It's the most beautiful example of gender equality in sport. We travel together to compete; we compete at the same time; we get the same kit, the same funding. But then you look at the make-up of the coaches, most of them are male. A lot of the management is male, but often when you're in it you don't question it. You accept that's how it is. Things just chug along until somebody points it out to you.

Now I'm in a position to challenge, and I've realized there's something wrong in a sport if we're not representative of the people we're helping. If we don't hear different voices how could we possibly know what it's like to deal with a female athlete like me, with a chaotic background who could miss testing? Maybe she needed more support to help her understand she didn't have to carry everything. Maybe her coach needed more support so she didn't have to work numerous jobs and coach in between. If we don't hear that variety of experience we can't understand those nuances.

Despite the highs and lows of her journey, Christine is still thankful for what sparked her imagination and led her to realize her dreams. For that she credits the sense of community around her East London home, the community who supported her in sport, and the open green spaces she was able to escape to to nurture her sense of adventure and indomitable spirit.

For kids like me, those are spaces where dreams are made. They are places where kids see possibilities. How many girls playing in fields or parks like that around the country are seeing themselves scoring a goal? Or running a gold-medal race? Or just pursuing sport because they love it? No one knows what dreams are made in those spaces. All I know is that they were so crucial in creating the person I am today.

CHAPTER 12

Building a Legacy

Baroness Tanni Grey-Thompson DBE

WHEELCHAIR RACER AND CROSS-BENCH PEER

*'As a campaigner I want to make sport accessible
and safe for every person... Sport at any level is
a powerful vehicle for inclusion and change.'*

In 2023, the visibility and perception of women in sport is at
an all-time high. There are female athletes themselves – past
and present – who have worked so hard to reach the top of
their game and to lay the foundations for a new generation of
sporting talent; there are those volunteers at the grassroots who
turn up in all kinds of weather to coach, train or support young
women wanting to play sport. Then, there are the leaders and
change-makers working to ensure that sport is accessible for
all, a safe environment to compete in and that women's voices

are heard. For Tanni Grey-Thompson – the former para-athlete turned parliamentarian – progress has been made but there's still an uphill battle to be won – one for which her twenty-five-year sporting career has stood her in good stead.

A few years ago I remember being at a parliamentary reception for football. One man came up to me and said, 'What you don't understand, Tanni, is that women don't really like football.' I replied, 'They don't? I thought they did...' He kept repeating that they didn't and that women didn't actually want to play. Apparently we were being forced to. I gave him three chances for a quiet chat outside the room, but he refused. In the end I had to tell him that the event was one of the most misogynistic events I'd ever been to and that far more respect was needed for women in sport. It's moments like that when you just have to say 'No'.

Challenging the status quo runs in Tanni's blood, and it's partly because of women like her, alongside trailblazers such as Baroness Sue Campbell who oversaw changes at the FA that laid the structural foundation for the Lionesses' success in 2022, that attitudes are shifting. It's the kind of determination that, on a smaller but no less important level, I have to thank my own mum for instilling in me. When I was banned from playing football for the boys' team aged ten, she knocked on the door of the FA in London to complain. She wanted me to have exactly the same opportunities as my brother. But whether the fight is local or, like Tanni's, played out in the corridors of power, I was interested in whether the playing field is levelling, in particular in Paralympic sport where Tanni dominated in wheelchair racing for sixteen years.

By her own admission, Tanni is not an athlete who wants to live on past glories. But to find the answer I wanted to understand more about her early years and her journey through elite Paralympic sport. Born with spina bifida, a condition where a baby's backbone does not form fully before birth, Tanni was paralysed from the waist down at the age of eight when her spinal cord severed. She credits her parents for instilling in her a fighting spirit which she put to use on, and now off, the track.

My dad was a strong feminist and he taught me how to deal with things. And I needed that because there was a lot of prejudice in the 1970s growing up with a disability. Both my parents were feisty in different ways. I remember being around five years old when I was walking with my mum and someone stopped me in the street to ask why my parents hadn't aborted me. Mum dealt with it, but she also sat me down to talk to me about abortion and why it was never a question for my parents.

As far as my disability was concerned they didn't make a big deal of it. They told me to get on with stuff. My dad was an architect but he refused to make our house wheelchair accessible. People thought he was being really mean, but he didn't want that house to be the only place where I could live. In many respects he was far ahead of his time.

And when I got my first wheelchair I thought it was amazing. I could run around and do whatever I wanted. And I was also very lucky too that my parents loved sports. My dad played cricket and my mum was obsessed with watching rugby so we were exposed to a lot of sports growing up.

Keen for Tanni to receive a decent education, her parents also fought for her to attend a mainstream secondary school in Wales at a time when disabled children were automatically segregated into special schools. It was there that her love of competitive sports developed. By the time she was enrolled into secondary school she was already swimming and horse riding, but the moment she tried out wheelchair racing she became hooked.

The special school that I could have gone to wasn't educating kids. It offered children a lower qualification called a CSE and if I was lucky I could sit a couple. In the end my parents threatened to sue the Secretary of State for Wales and I was sent to the only school in South Glamorgan that accepted wheelchair users. By the time I'd left I had ten O levels and four A levels and I went on to university. I think social justice was around me before I had any idea of what it actually was.

My dad was also really keen that I did a range of sports. He wanted me to be active and learn those skills. I played some basketball and table tennis. Again, he was ahead of his time in terms of encouraging multi-sport. But I remember coming fourth in my first wheelchair race at the age of twelve and thinking, 'This is amazing.' I already moved 100 miles an hour in my day chair, but this was different. This was about competing. Nerves were rushing through me and there was 100 metres of concrete track ahead of me. I was flying. At that moment I became obsessed.

But the chances of seeing women participating in disability sport were close to zero at that time. Even the Paralympic Games, which evolved from the rehabilitation of war veterans and civilians after the Second World War, hadn't introduced women into competition until 1960 – now considered the first Paralympic Games as we know it. At that Games, the British team fielded eighteen men and thirteen women with the first women's gold medal won in archery by Margaret Maughan, who had been paralysed from the waist down in a road accident. As for reaching a wider audience, the first televised Paralympics didn't happen in the UK until 1980 – when Tanni was eleven years old – when the BBC broadcast a one-hour special from the Arnhem Games in the Netherlands. Given that lack of visibility I was fascinated about whom Tanni looked to for inspiration.

Seeing someone disabled on TV was massive. Not only did you rarely see disabled people on TV, you didn't see them out and about either. The only representation I saw of someone who was paralysed and in a wheelchair was Ironside, the main character in the US drama of the same name, and Sandy Richardson who starred in the UK soap opera Crossroads. *But these were non-disabled actors playing disabled parts, so I knew it wasn't real.*

But there was a Welsh athlete called Chris Hallam and I remember watching him on TV competing in the London Marathon. Chris was real, and seeing him was fantastic. He was a larger-than-life character. He had dyed blond hair and an outrageous taste in leopard-print body suits. He was loud and rude and later he would become an amazing friend. He'd crashed his motorbike and became a wheelchair user, but he wouldn't allow anyone to patronize him. He broke down so many attitudinal barriers around disability but he also set a very high standard for athletic performance. He set out to shatter the view that disabled people were just 'having a go'.

From school sports, Tanni progressed to her first sports club and got her first coach when she was fifteen. She joined Bridgend Athletics Club, twenty-five miles from her home in Cardiff. The volunteer coach there, Roy Anthony, knew nothing about wheelchair racing, but was prepared to take Tanni on at a time when wheelchair racing wasn't perceived as 'proper' athletics. It is Roy she credits with instilling in her a training discipline that never left her during her career.

Roy needed a knighthood for coaching twenty hormonal teenage girls. He was a police officer who joked that he went to work for a rest. He was the person who taught me how to train. In the winter in Bridgend we used to train in the multi-storey car park. We'd sprint up and down the ramps and Roy would say very calmly, 'Right, girls. You can't shout at the drivers who just want to park their car in the car park.' They were always getting in the way but we had to let them in. At that point I had an idea that I wanted to take sport further, but I'm not sure other people thought I was talented enough. There were other girls who were better than me, but what I learned during that time was how to train.

Ask all athletes, and they will say the same. Ten per cent of success is about natural talent. Ninety per cent is the hard graft needed to hone that talent. And it was Tanni's dedication to training that paid off when she won her first notable title aged sixteen competing in the 100 metres wheelchair race at the Junior National Games. A year later she was selected for the Welsh national squad. How did that feel?

I raced in a competition in Liverpool, between special schools from across the country. I won my event, but one girl who had been really strong didn't compete that day and afterwards one of the teachers told me that's the reason I'd won. The following week it was the national juniors and the girl was there. Not only did I beat her but I broke the junior record for the 100 metres. Suddenly people said, 'Oh, you're really good.' That was amazing.

When I was invited to join the national squad a year later, that felt incredibly exciting because now it wasn't just Roy or my parents who thought I had some talent. It was a different kind of confirmation.

Tanni continued to raise the bar, success she attributes to that training discipline, the seeds of which were sown at Bridgend. The need for dedication is something young people must be aware of if they have any chance of reaching Paralympian standard, she says. Perhaps controversially, it's a reason why she struggles with the word 'Parasport' which is now applied to all disability sport regardless of level. Admittedly, until our interview I'd not considered that when I go into schools to talk to children about the power of sport, I encourage them to be fit and active rather than promising they'll reach Olympic or Paralympic medal standard – a tiny percentage of any sporting reality. But don't all young hopefuls need inspiration to encourage them to the next level?

Yes they do and I understand the reasons for calling all disability sport Parasport because of the strength of the Paralympic movement and its branding, but the danger is that it gives young people the wrong impression of where they might end up. Now you're called a Para if you're a Paralympian, you're on a Para performance pathway or if you're a disabled child doing sport every six weeks. Yet we don't call non-disabled children who do sport every six weeks an Oly-athlete. So already Olympian and Paralympian sport is being treated differently, and it feeds the idea that disabled people competing at the elite level are somehow lesser, or that being a Paralympian is easier. For me, that's discriminatory. People think that discrimination is all about accessibility but it's far more complicated than that. I feel it should be called disability sport or at the lower levels just sport.

The hard fact is that if you train once a week you are not going to become a Paralympian. You need to be training twelve times a week and even then, it's really hard. So for me that word Parasport reinforces a view around disabled sportspeople: that somehow you could be a non-disabled person competing at county level, then become disabled and suddenly you'll be a Paralympian, but it doesn't work that way.

The difficulty is that you need the magic fairy dust – it's finding a balance between inspiring young people to get to the next level and for them to understand the reality. Certain things will be expected from them. Elite sport is not warm and cuddly. You can't just turn up and train when you want.

In fact, Tanni's training schedule over the majority of her competitive career was a punishing twice a day, six days a week and fifty weeks of the year. After she left school and began studying at Loughborough University, she was also training alongside completing her degree in politics and social administration. Those years were to become the making of her, she explains, but not always for the right reasons.

There were many good athletes at Loughborough but very few disabled athletes. It was a pretty harsh regime at the time and if you made it through the system you became a really strong athlete, but it wasn't because of its athlete-centred approach. The gym where I did circuit training wasn't accessible, so I had to get out of my chair and crawl up steps and drag my chair up to get to it. I couldn't access the track because getting a key to unlock the gate to get on to the track was hard to do. Again, I had to get out of my chair, crawl up the steps, drag my chair through the pavilion and crawl down a grassy bank. It didn't occur to anyone in the athletics club to help, but also underlying that there was a view from some that disability sport didn't have any value.

In the end I trained with the mountaineering club. They were brilliant. A couple of the guys would always meet me and carry my chair up the steps. They didn't care as long as I turned up and did my best. Then, when I started training out on the road on my own that made me far stronger and quicker.

Tanni describes wheelchair racing as being closer to cycling than athletics. Key to success in the sport is precision technique under pressure. And when it comes to pushing, each competitor's style is dependent on many factors including an athlete's specific disability. By training with the mountaineering group, Tanni built up her upper body strength, crucial to a racer's sprint speed.

There's an assumption that you push a race chair like a day chair, but it's totally different. With a race chair, you don't grab the rim at all. Your hand essentially punches the rim at around 10 o'clock if you imagine a clock face.

When you're flat out pushing you're in contact with the push rim for just over 0.1 seconds at top speeds, so technique is really important because it's all about how you transfer your power through the rim. My race weight was 45 kilos, which was my optimal power-to-weight ratio. Positioning – where you sit over the axle and your knee height – is also crucial to get right. I spent a lot of time working on that. I had a treadmill in the garage that my wheelchair could fit on and I practised a lot of technique on there.

But I was fortunate that I learned at a young age to push well. If you learn to push badly you can break those habits during training, but it's really hard to break them when you are under extreme pressure and your heart rate is 198. Anyone can train hard, but you also have to train smart, and I was pretty methodical about it.

Also key is an athlete's racing chair. Gears or levers are not permitted on racing chairs, however each chair can be customized to fit every competitor. When wheelchair racing first appeared in the Paralympic programme in 1960, chair designs were relatively basic, but since the 1980s race wheelchairs have developed rapidly alongside the materials used to create them, making them more lightweight and aerodynamic.

Your equipment is everything. And your chair is transported on a different bus than you are. I remember when my daughter was around six years old, I announced that I would rather have put my child on a different bus than my racing chair. Obviously I was joking, but the anxiety of flying or being transported and your chair not turning up or being damaged was very real. I spent much of my competitive career in a constant panic.

I changed my chair around once a year. My husband Ian (who was also Tanni's coach) was a scientist so we looked at things in a scientific way. I was very specific about what I wanted and if I was getting a new chair it was important for me to be there. Some company owners were more in favour of that than others, but designers often loved that interaction and challenge. It was about getting the best piece of equipment I could and once it arrived I'd check it, measure it and do a session in it.

I remember I had one chair made before the Athens Olympics, but it came back heavier than I wanted so I left Ian in the garage sawing parts of the wheel guard off. It was around two months before I was due to compete. I was so anxious I couldn't watch.

Tanni would go on to dominate internationally in the 100, 200, 400 and 800 metre disciplines, starting with a bronze medal at the Seoul Olympics in 1988. In Barcelona she became the first woman to break the 60-second barrier for 400 metres. In total over five Paralympic Games her medal haul reached eleven golds, four silvers and one bronze alongside five golds, four silvers and three bronzes at World Championships. Following in the footsteps of her friend Chris Hallam she also claimed victory in the 1992 London Wheelchair Marathon and went on to win six more times over her career. Yet despite winning medals for sprints, Tanni in fact preferred longer distances.

The 1500 and the 5000 were the races I loved most because those were a lot more tactical. I trained with guys on the track and they pushed me all over, they nudged me out of lanes and boxed me in so I'd have to find a way out. It meant that I had loads of experience of racing those tough races. So, when it came to racing in the women's race I knew exactly what to do.

But at the end of the day, the Paralympics is about medals and I had more chance of winning a gold at the Paralympics in the 400 and 800 metres. The 1500 and above is tactical, but technically I was a better sprinter and in wheelchair racing that's 100, 200, 400 and 800 metres and my biggest strength was being able to push very quickly once I was at top speed, so those were the distances I mainly ended up competing in.

Having trained with men myself at around the age of sixteen, I understand how it made me a better hockey player. Some were afraid to tackle me, but most didn't hold back. Many were stronger and faster and it pushed my physical strength and tactical ability to the limits. And in the run-up to any competition – in particular the Olympics – it was my physical fitness that I mainly doubted. When it came to the moment of competition, however, I was always confident I'd done everything possible to deal with what was thrown at me. I wondered whether Tanni ever felt debilitating run-up nerves.

In training I was always very chatty, but on race day I couldn't speak to anyone. I was sick for about two hours before a race. I couldn't eat. I used to be at a track several hours beforehand. The team didn't always love me for that, but I would have rather been on the track throwing up than being sick on the bus.

I think it was mostly fear of not being good enough or not doing the best I could. Also going round in my head would have been thoughts about my warm-up, the race tactics and then there are other things like the temperature of the track, how sticky it is, and the wind direction. I had to have my own methodical process.

Once I was at the start line I was fine and there are a handful of races I remember where it was a perfect day, I was in the best shape, and everything clicked. Barcelona felt easy but it wasn't easy. But it was one of those competitions when I hit that sweet spot – I went into each race with a lot of confidence. I knew I was in good shape and that doesn't happen very often in your career.

Added to the pressure of any race, Tanni also competed at a time when elite Paralympic sport still needed to fight for its place on the world stage, always in danger of being perceived as a sideshow. When she looks back now, how far does she believe Paralympic sport has come in both recognition and coverage?

Things have definitely got better but there's a way to go. In 1988 in Seoul, a separate village was built for the Paralympics because they didn't think people would buy the flats in the Olympic village if disabled people had been staying in them. Their attitude wasn't great.

Barcelona in 1992 was better. Whereas before you may have competed in a near-empty stadium, tickets were sold at reasonable prices so people who didn't get tickets for the Olympics all came to support the Games. For me, having a crowd never changed the way I raced, but it's nice to have something at the beginning and end to feed off.

In Atlanta in 1996 the Olympic village was being dismantled around us as we moved in. The US didn't get the Paralympics at all, which was weird because in the US the American Disability Act is an amazing piece of legislation. There have also been scholarships for disabled athletes since the 1960s. Since then the US has stepped up, but the coverage is still not as good as here.

By Sydney in 2000 there was coverage every night on the BBC and since 2012 there has been dedicated coverage on Channel 4. But the coverage of Para-sport in between games is still not good and the sponsorship and money is still terrible.

Of the coverage itself, there's also a tendency to cover Paralympic sport differently. If I'm honest, some of it is a bit uncomfortable. There's this idea that sportspeople are inspirational simply because they are disabled. It's called 'inspiration porn' – that people are amazing, brave, incredible and wonderful because of their disability. Of course there are inspirational moments and inspirational sportspeople, and some Para-athletes do have dramatic life-changing stories, but I was paralysed aged eight and I don't remember much about it. I did sport and I happen to be disabled. To me or my family it really wasn't a big deal.

Undoubtedly the profile of Paralympic sport has been raised further since 2012. The 2022 Commonwealth Games in Birmingham, for example, showcased the largest ever integrated disabled and non-disabled programme in the history of the Games. Para-sport had been a part of the Games since 1994, however it wasn't until the Manchester Games in 2002 that Para-athletes were fully integrated into their national teams and contributed to a nation's medal tally. Given this development, I was interested to hear Tanni's views on whether, as a result, she believes that the increased awareness of Paralympic sport and increased visibility of its athletes has had the knock-on effect of creating a better understanding of disability in society.

In terms of sport, it's definitely improved. Before 2012 there was some research done which asked people to name a Paralympian. It was just about my name and that was it. That was brilliant for my ego, but the reality is that for the Games to be successful we had to sell a lot of tickets. To do that we needed names and the public needed to know who they were coming to watch. I was retired so it's really great now that there are so many more Paralympians who are known names: Ellie Simmonds, Sarah Storey, Jonnie Peacock and Sophie Christiansen to name a few.

The integration of sport has also improved, and what is being done at the Commonwealth Games could certainly be done at World Championships. Combining Olympic and Paralympic Games would require combining events for 16,000 athletes and it may just be too big for any one city.

As for wider awareness, 2012 was an amazing Games, but it didn't fix life for disabled people at all. Only half of disabled people who can work in this country are in work and a headteacher can still exclude a child on account that they are disabled. Disability hate crime has risen, although some of that is down to increased reporting. Personally, I am treated in one of three ways: as an athlete, as a parliamentarian and as a disabled person and it's in that last category that I experience the most discrimination.

The Games are amazing, but don't expect them to fix every problem in the world. And to say that they change the lives of disabled people is like saying that because 2012 showcased women's talent, it changed women's lives. It didn't. I don't want the next generation of women to be fighting for the same things I was, but I would argue misogyny is worse than it ever was. In sport and in public life you are told you shouldn't have an opinion because you're a woman. I think for sportswomen,

social media is really hard right now because if you have
an opinion then the level of threat and abuse you receive is
pretty high.

And it's in public life where Tanni now concentrates most of her
time. In 2010 she entered the House of Lords as a cross-bench
peer, but in truth, she says, she had been planning her steps
out of sport since the age of twenty-one, a long-term outlook
she adopted early on that I found surprising, albeit wise. So
many athletes don't get support given to them at the end of
their career, and what is provided is still very limited given it's
such a hard transition to make. You may be funded for a short
while or have some help with a first job interview or a CV, but
after that ex-athletes are on their own. I wondered how Tanni's
sporting career helped her in her second life.

Towards the end of my career I was starting to get injured a
lot and I was tired and my body was broken. I'd also had my
daughter by then and I didn't want to travel. But the reality
was I'd always thought about that moment. Ever since I'd
started competing, I'd been fortunate to have my dad saying
to me, 'Tanni. What are you going to do when you grow up?'
The question was always what I was going to do when I left
sport and I didn't want to be one of those athletes who was
always looking back.

Nothing replaces the feeling of competing, but I also don't
want it to. I wanted something to fill that gap, so from 2004,

I started planning my steps out. Many athletes assume there is going to be a job in the media for them, but the reality is that happens to very few people. You need to have other things in your life. I always enjoyed doing other stuff because it gave me a balance to my sport. I sat on the National Disability Council which oversaw the implementation of the Disability Discrimination Act in Wales and that fitted around my training. It meant that I came to training really fresh because I was thinking about other stuff.

Now in my parliamentary career, there are a lot of similarities. I trained hard for twenty-five years, but my time on the track during the Paralympic Games was a total of 19.5 minutes. I learned from a young age that to get to do good stuff, you have to do a lot of very boring stuff. In sport, that boring stuff was training. In politics I spend a vast amount of time reading briefing papers. Sport taught me that there are no easy wins. You have no right to win. At the end of the day if you do that's nice, but all you can do is prepare yourself in the best way you can.

One of Tanni's notable wins has been her campaign to extend to the world of sport existing legislation that protects under-18s from abuse by people in positions of trust. By closing a legal loophole it means that any person in a sports organisation, such as a coach, cannot legally have a sexual relationship with any minor in their care. The legislation applies to everyone – male and female – and builds on previous pioneering work, for example that done by the late Professor Celia Brackenridge OBE, a former sportswoman herself who campaigned tirelessly for the protection of children in sport.

And while the legislation also applies to both disabled and non-disabled people, it is worth noting that although little research has been carried out into abuse of Para-athletes, the International Olympic Committee estimates that competitors may be up to four times more likely to be victimized or abused, whether that's verbally, physically or sexually. I know myself how pushing your mind and body to the limit exposes vulnerability, although thankfully I have never been a victim of abuse. I wondered how clear-cut abuse is in sport, and how easy it was for Tanni to lobby for that change.

There are times in sport when what constitutes abuse is debatable. For example, I had one athlete complain to me that a coach had asked for a training diary, and that they thought this was abuse. That's not abuse. Being told you're not training hard enough in elite sport is not abuse. Being asked to turn up to a training session is not abuse. It's your job. Elite sport is very hard and anyone going down that path will have to deal with hard truths, but there is other stuff going on that is abuse and must never be tolerated.

Yet when it came to the positions of trust legislation, there were a lot of people in sport who didn't want that change in the legislation. It was often argued to me that sports coaches were never in relationships with sixteen- or seventeen-year-

olds. People said it didn't happen, but that's not true and it's
unbelievable to me that it wasn't illegal before.

What's hard is that you have these amazing moments in
sport that are incredible, but sport also has a bit of a dark
side. For me it's very simple. If you are a coach and you are
in a relationship with someone on the team then you absent
yourself.

In the end I didn't have to deliver the speech I'd prepared in
the House of Lords, because there was overwhelming support
for the bill. I'd spent the best part of four years preparing it,
and it was probably the best speech of my entire life. It was
powerful. Of course, there's a part of me that would have
loved to have delivered it, but in that scenario what was more
important was getting the right result – winning was about
learning when to step up and learning when to step back.

Tanni is now campaigning for mandatory reporting of suspected
abuse by people who have contact with young people in a
sporting environment. She also wants to make illegal coercive
relationships in sport, a piece of legislation she admits may be
more difficult to get over the line.

In elite sport you are vulnerable because there are people in
positions of power and coercive relationships do happen. I've
seen the evidence and there's lots of it. I remember one female
athlete telling me about a coach who told her she could make
the team, but there were things she had to do for him. But if

that woman complained, the coach may say he was just offering her an extra coaching session. Ongoing revelations across many sports have also shown these types of relationships happen to boys too. It's hard to prove, but it's happening, and we shouldn't pretend it isn't.

As for encouraging more women into sport at the grassroots, Tanni believes that sporty boys are still valued more than sporty girls at school and that while a shift is happening, much more work needs to be done.

The reasons are complex, but from a young age boys are encouraged to kick a ball, whereas girls are often seen on the sidelines. Women enjoy being active – everything we are seeing in women's sport at the moment affirms that – but real women being active is still a self-conscious thing for so many girls and women. We are worried about so much; from how we are judged to what happens if we lose. But women's role models need not be Olympian or Paralympian athletes but just females doing sport: whether that's a friend at school, or a teacher, or someone in the community.

As a campaigner I want to make sport accessible and safe for every person. Whatever a person's sporting journey turns out to be, all sporting journeys must start somewhere. There are tremendous financial pressures and tough decisions that need to be taken all the time, something I see constantly in politics, but lots of physical activity doesn't have to cost. What you do need is an open, safe space. We also need to keep building a positive narrative around all sport, especially women's sport. Sport at any level is a powerful vehicle for inclusion and change. It's also tremendous fun.

Sam Quek MBE

When I started working on this book, I had in my mind a selection of elite women athletes whom I greatly admired. Some of these I knew from past Olympics or world competition – names imprinted in my mind from when I was a girl growing up in Merseyside; other women competed around the same time as me and I admired them as contemporaries, and some are a new generation whom I've cheered on from my living room or from the studio. Many of these women I've now welcomed on to *Question of Sport*.

But admiring people from afar is nothing like getting up close and personal for an in-depth interview. The time and effort women took to talk to me for this book with such amazing candour took me by surprise at every turn. Each of their stories is different but each interview touched on every aspect of what it takes to succeed as a woman in sport: the challenges; the setbacks; the knife-edge decisions; the life-changing and sometimes life-threatening moments; the sheer determination to keep going; the breathtaking elation of winning. I could relate to so many of those career milestones plus the tumult of feelings that run alongside, but each interview also left me with many jaw-dropping moments – it turned out I didn't know the richness of these women's experiences as well as I thought, and I absolutely loved listening to every single one.

At a time when momentum is building around women's sport, I hope that these interviews will serve as a barometer for how far we've come, but also a reminder of how far we need to go. From the experiences of my oldest interviewee, footballer Sheila Parker, to my youngest, skateboarder Sky Brown, I was struck by the freedom women are now starting to feel to be themselves, to feel proud of what they are achieving and to let nothing stand in their way. But we must keep pushing.

Not every woman is going to stand on an Olympic podium, but women embedding sport into their lives for the sheer love of it is something I hope readers of this book will feel inspired to do, whatever your age. For girls who do want to pursue a sporting career, all the women in this book started at the grassroots. It's where dreams are made, but we have to ensure that those dreams can be realized for everybody regardless of wealth, ethnicity, sexual orientation or disability. Women's sport needs investment, energy and support behind it at every stage – not just when medals are won, but consistently and over time from the school gym and the local playing fields right through to the world's stadiums and elite competition. All the women who came before me helped me succeed, and I hope these stories have inspired you in the same way. My life has been enriched through sport in more ways than I can imagine. We all deserve the same opportunity to reach our potential.

Acknowledgements

Helena Drakakis: You have been immense in helping me put this together. In truth, without your level of effort, it wouldn't have been possible. Thank you so much!

Gabby Logan: A true on-screen trailblazer and someone who I have looked up to and still do. Thank you for your kind words and being part of the movement that sporting women are trying to achieve.

Paula Radcliffe: I always knew that to be the best, one had to push and go to a place physically and mentally very few can go. After speaking to you for this book, I didn't know there was a level beyond that – you really are one of a kind.

Amy Williams: Thank you for your raw honesty and speaking so boldly about your journey. Your competitiveness and desire to always be better is something I will always find incredibly inspiring.

Dame Katherine Grainger: May everyone strike the right balance of warmth, steeliness and honesty as you do. A true inspiration to not just elite athletes but those whose paths you cross every day.

Dame Sarah Storey: Your success and medals speak for themselves but the dedication and will to commit everything to get there is something not many would do. As a mum to another mum, you inspire me that anything is possible.

Fatima Whitbread: I loved every minute we spoke for this book. Your story took me through so many emotions and opened my mind to many more things. I'm so glad this book enabled us to become friends.

Sky Brown: Your energy is so infectious, and I love how positively you see the world. At such a young age the world is your oyster and I thoroughly look forward to seeing you thrive and achieve more great things. You know where I am if you ever need anything!

Shaunagh Brown: You are a massive inspiration when it comes to being yourself and being the best version of you. Your will to be bold and talk about what is right is something our world needs more of.

Sheila Parker: The epitome of living and breathing football. You quite simply paved the way for all females involved in the game and without you the game would not have reached the height it has today. You're a true footballing heroine.

Kate Richardson-Walsh: Courageous, kind, fair and funny – thank you for being such a key feature in my sporting journey. Your dedication over the years to give everyone a voice, both in women's sport and the LGBTQ+ community, has been game-changing and I'm proud to call you my friend.

Rebecca Adlington: Your journey to reaching the heights of your success, to where you are now, is just amazing, yet you are one of the humblest people I know. You are quite simply an incredible role model and legend of swimming.

Christine Ohuruogu: Listening to your story just screams of understated excellence. You're a girl after my own heart when it comes to competitiveness and family. Thank you for being so open and talking so honestly about what needs to change.

Dame Tanni Grey-Thompson: I could sit and listen, discuss and debate all day with you and I'm so glad I got to know more about you and story. Thank you for all you are doing to change sport on all levels, for the good.